Guided
by
Angels

THERE ARE NO GOODBYES

Guided
by
Angels

My tour of the spirit world

Paddy McMahon

Collins

This paperback edition published in 2011

First published in 2010 by Collins
HarperCollins Publishers
77–85 Fulham Palace Road
London W6 8JB

www.harpercollins.co.uk

13 12 11 10
9 8 7 6 5 4 3 2 1

Text © Paddy McMahon 2010, 2011

The author asserts his moral right to be
identified as the author of this work

A catalogue record for this book is
available from the British Library

ISBN: 978-0-00-743488-6

Printed and bound in Great Britain by
Clays Ltd, St Ives plc

Mixed Sources
Product group from well-managed
forests and other controlled sources
www.fsc.org Cert no. SW-COC-001806
© 1996 Forest Stewardship Council

FSC

FSC is a non-profit international organisation established to promote the
responsible management of the world's forests. Products carrying the FSC
label are independently certified to assure consumers that they come
from forests that are managed to meet the social, economic and
ecological needs of present and future generations.

Find out more about HarperCollins and the environment at
www.harpercollins.co.uk/green

Minds are like parachutes – they only function
when open.

Thomas Dewey

Contents

Have you ever wondered …

Is there life after death?
If so, where do people go when they die?
Can you keep in contact with your loved ones?
Are they able to help you?
Will you meet them again?

You'll find the answers to these and many more questions
in the following pages.

Acknowledgements

There's a host of people that I'd like to thank for their friend-ship and support over many years, but I'll have to be selective and beg for forgiveness from those I'm omitting.

My special thanks to:
My wonderful agent and friend, Marianne Gunn O'Connor, without whose encouragement and enthusiasm I wouldn't have embarked on this book at all.

Jenny Heller, of HarperCollins, for her enabling role in the publication of the book and for her unfailing courtesy and kindness.

Moira Reilly, also of HarperCollins, whose championing of the book has been of immense importance to me.

Gill Paul, for her comprehensive editing.

Pat Lynch, for his unfailing, cheerful helpfulness.

My sister, Teresa, and my friends, Catherine, Agnes, Andy, Isabel, Martina, Tony, John, Michel, Jim; and Armen, who designed and manages my web site and has been supportive in countless other ways.

And Maura, to whom I owe inexpressible gratitude for so much, including the fact that, but for her, I wouldn't have discovered until too late, if at all, that I had a seriously progressive health condition, and I'm still here to tell the tale.

Introduction

If there is one thing of which we can all be certain, it's the fact that we are going to die. At my age (76) most of my contemporaries are already gone.

In my early 20s there were five of us – a group who used to meet regularly every Saturday for years and often during the week, as we were all involved in theatrical activities of some kind. We kept in contact, although it became sporadic as circumstances and family responsibilities took over. Four of the five are gone now, and I'm the last man standing, so to speak. And I'm not standing all that firmly, so my turn will inevitably come in the not-too-distant future.

Many of my friends and acquaintances died suddenly, and for no obvious health reasons. One man died watching television, another asleep in his bed and another playing golf. One of my friends died eating his breakfast. These are mundane activities that somehow sparked the end of a life, and I could quote many more examples. Some people that I knew died in car crashes or accidents; some committed suicide. Some of those deaths were tragic shocks; others were expected, after months or even years of illness. In some of them, old age was the obvious cause. As it will be for many of us.

In 1977, shortly before my life changed in ways that I will describe in this book, I remember looking at the body of one of my friends, Tadhg Murray, as he lay silent and cold in his coffin. He had been a very vivid, articulate man, who carried his theatrical interests into the way he related to the world. There was nothing flamboyant about him in dress or appearance, but he managed to bring a sense of colour to his descriptions of even the most humdrum of happenings. He was a gentle and very popular man, much in demand as an actor and director in amateur-dramatic circles.

As I stood looking sadly – and with an almost overwhelming feeling of loss – at his now lifeless body, it made no sense to me that all that animation would be no more. Surely the death of his body just couldn't be the end of his life, which had impacted so profoundly on all who knew him?

Less than six months after that I was introduced to a whole new world – and I didn't even have to leave my body to experience it! Because of the events that transpired then, I no longer have any fear of death. I accepted totally the continuity of life, because I was given extensive information about what happens to the departing soul in the immediate aftermath of the death of the body – and how the mindset it carries affects subsequent developments. Most important, it has been a great comfort and joy for me to learn of the help that's available to each and every soul on its passing – according to its readiness to receive help.

Fear plays a major role in all of our lives; in fact, it's unlikely that there is – or ever has been – a human being who has not known fear. Fear takes many forms, and in many ways it guides our lives. We fear the unknown, and a potential crisis around the corner; we are afraid of being thought foolish or ridiculous, or being laughed at if we express a point of view. We fear punishment (both temporal and eternal) if we fail to live up to expectations; we also fear not being loved, not being able to love and even being unable to show love in order to experience happiness. We are frightened about being unemployable, not managing financially, losing control of our mental or physical faculties, through such things as senility or accidents; we are fearful of the future, and what will happen to our children when we are not around to help them grow up to be happy and successful. And that's just the tip of the iceberg. Life is challenging for human beings on a daily basis, without even considering the fear of death. To some extent, this is the fear that overrides all other fears, and is, perhaps, the foundation upon which all other fears are based.

The word 'death' implies an ending. In between our birth and our death there are all sorts of endings, such as relationships, employment, and even mental or physical capacity. These are deaths of sorts; although not so final as the death of our bodies, they still represent the death of something that was vital and alive.

We fear death not just because we have experienced these smaller deaths as we progress through our lives, and therefore dread the possibility that there could be something worse; we fear death because it is the unknown.

What happens to us when we die is something about which we are all curious. Some people believe that when we're dead 'that's it'. Others believe that we go on – but to what? Either way we're unsure what death holds, and this strikes a chord of fear in the very heart of our beings.

This book provides answers not just to what happens when we die, but to many other questions as well. The main object of the book is to help people go through existence on earth secure in the knowledge that life continues towards complete freedom of spirit – and that there's no reason whatsoever to be afraid of death. I hope it will have an incidental effect of helping to make life easier for everyone, including, ideally, freeing us from fear, generally.

My life and the way I live it changed entirely when I discovered that we all have guardian angels/spirit guides that are available and willing to help us in all aspects of our lives, if we so wish. Some of these guides are loved ones who have passed over; others are souls at an advanced level of consciousness who want to help all others who are not yet at that stage. All are familiar with life and its challenges, and are, therefore, in a position to guide us through the minefield of potential worries that inhibit our lives.

I have been on a momentous, life-changing journey in which I have developed active communication with my own guides over many years. In this book I'll share details of that journey, with suggestions as to how others may be helped in achieving their own communication, if they so wish.

I think that one of the greatest things about life is the fact that we all have our own individual styles – we have our own way of doing things, and our own outlook on life. Our guides can help and encourage us in anything we choose to do, in whatever way we choose to do it. In no way do they impose on our free will; in fact, they encourage and help us to find our ideal form of self-expression. Spirit guides, or guardian angels as you may like to call them, are not magicians, and they do not have a 'one size fits all' approach to living. The ways they can help us are manifold, and the philosophy I have developed – and expanded, through individual consultations, workshops, talks and writing – is based on encouraging people to find and be comfortable with their lives and their individual style of living.

This book has been inspired by my communication with a soul who has acted as a spirit guide for me throughout my life – although I did not even become aware of it until I was in my 40s. Other guides have made significant contributions to the philosophy of life that suits me, and I have filtered the details of that philosophy throughout the book.

I feel deeply privileged to have survived long enough to be able to share this information with those of you who may be drawn to read it, and I hope that it may help you to see the apparent conundrum of life and death in a light-hearted and wholly reassuring way.

Paddy McMahon

Chapter 1

How My Life Changed

As a child, an adolescent, and even into early adulthood, fear of death was more or less my constant companion. Not my own death – but that of my father.

I was born in 1933 in a rural location in County Clare, Ireland, the third of seven children. There was a sort of magical, mystical aura to the place where I grew up; the existence of ghosts and fairies was taken for granted, and the pathways that led to their fairy forts were out of bounds for walking on or even crossing. I don't remember being told about all of that; it was simply part of the folklore of the place. When I was a child I firmly believed that crossing a path or walking through a fairy fort would bring bad luck. In fact, until the age of 10 or 11 my life was dictated to an extent by the promise of good or bad luck, depending upon my actions. Even as a young adult I didn't consider my beliefs 'supernatural'. It was just the way things were. From an early age I was accustomed to the idea that there were two worlds – physical and non-physical. As a result it has never been a huge leap for me to believe that there may be something other than what we see around us.

Storytelling was a feature of the rural location in which I was raised. An old man – I thought he was old, but he was probably much younger than I am now – who lived about a quarter of a mile from my first childhood home had a seemingly endless repertoire of stories, and I spent many a rapt evening listening to him. The fact that a lot of them were ghost stories made them even more enthralling for me – except that in order to get home I had to travel along a dark boreen (a little road) with bushes on each side of it. I was perpetually convinced that a ghost was going to jump out from behind every bush. But that didn't stop me from going back repeatedly for more stories.

The religious ethos of my childhood was extremely orthodox Catholic. Heaven beckoned to those who were pure and truly good; Purgatory was the destination for those of us who were a mixture of good and bad. Hell, however, was for those who had committed even one mortal sin, and it was there that they would burn in hellfire for all eternity. My father had given up practising religion when I was about 6 years old, and I was terrified that he was going to end up in Hell. I firmly believed that the one and only way to escape eternal punishment in Hell was by making a confession to a priest, who was God's representative, and expressing true contrition for all sins, thus earning God's forgiveness. Without religion, my father could not be released from his sins and he would not be spared. The thought of this – and his likely fate – haunted me.

In contrast to my father, my mother was extremely religious. So was I. I used to worry a lot about what happened to people when they died – no doubt influenced by my concern for my father.

One element of my religious conditioning was completely untainted by fear. Guardian angels were a constant reality for me as a child, and when things were at their darkest I felt that they were always there to help me. I didn't have any picture of guardian angels in my mind. I just thought of them as loving beings flying around helping people. I didn't think about whether they had once been real-life people. I didn't give them much thought at all. But their loving presence and my belief in their ability to guide me through my life – and protect me and those around me – was an important part of my childhood. Each night, before I fell asleep, I used to ask them to mind me – and everybody else in my family. My usual 'prayer' was: 'Angel of God, my guardian dear, to whom God's love commits me here, ever this day be at my side, to light and guard, to rule and guide. Amen.' It became almost a ritual for me to repeat this prayer each night.

In 1952 I got a job as an executive officer in the Irish Civil Service in Dublin, and that Christmas I headed home to County Clare to be with my family. After the festivities were over, my father accompanied me to the bus that would take me back to Dublin. It was then that I had my first memorable psychic experience. Although, to me, he had no obvious appearance of illness, as I said goodbye to him I knew with an inner certainty that I would not see him alive again. What's more, I knew that he knew, too. I resolved that I would write him a long letter, saying all the things that I had always wanted to say but had never been able to. I wanted to tell him how much I loved him. But I had not yet put pen to paper when I got a call, in February 1953, to tell me that he had died after a brief illness.

I sat by my father's bed, by his body, all night long. I didn't do this for any traditional religious reasons; I simply wanted to. I felt deep regret that I had not written that letter to him. As I sat there, I recalled how affectionate he had been towards my siblings and me as children, and I experienced an almost unbearable feeling of sadness. Other people came and went during the night, only staying briefly. They commented upon how peaceful he looked. I wondered where he was and what was happening to him. I knew there had been no obvious deathbed repentance and it was hard to contemplate that even as I sat beside his still body his soul might be undergoing the unimaginable punishment of hellfire. I wished I could have talked to him more freely, particularly about my ever-present concern for his eternal salvation.

My father's passing had a cataclysmic impact on me, and began the process that would eventually lead to an entire change in my consciousness. I couldn't imagine what eternity would be like. I hoped, rather than believed, that I would see him again, but I didn't have any idea how that might happen. I felt bereft and confused, but still hopeful that we would meet again. Physical experience doesn't prepare us for a concept of endlessness; however, even within my limited grasp of the concept I reasoned that there was hope for him. As the span of a human lifetime could be no more than a mini-second in eternity, its deeds couldn't justly be judged in eternal terms – no matter how sinful those deeds might be considered. I moved away from the orthodox belief structures with which I had grown up, and resolved that I'd try never to allow my thinking to be controlled by fear or dogmas or institutions built on foundations of fear.

I returned to Dublin, troubled and distressed by the passing of my father. But life has a habit of carrying on, no matter how deeply traumatised we become, and so it was with mine. I continued working in the Civil Service, got involved in amateur acting and directing, and began dabbling in writing. I got married, became a father of two children, a boy and a girl, and settled into domesticity and the furtherance of my career. I cast to the back of my mind the psychic experience that had preceded my father's death. My only other memorable psychic experience was a dream that a horse called Never Say Die would win the English Derby. It did. I'm afraid I didn't trust the dream enough to place a bet of more than a few shillings, and

I've never had a dream like that since (deservedly so because of my lack of trust!). Later, I thought of the dream as a sort of a cosmic joke, foreshadowing subsequent developments for me.

My mother died in 1974 when I was 40. She was a wonderful woman who was a genius at managing to keep the whole household ticking over reasonably smoothly during an era when money was very scarce. In mourning her, I deeply regretted that her life hadn't been easier. My grief for her, however, was much more straightforward. I did not fear what might happen to her after she died, as I had with my father. His death had been the catalyst for change, and at that stage I had shed all the fear-based orthodox belief structures of my youth. I was open to new ideas – at the most instinctive level.

One day in 1978, when I was in my early 40s, I visited the public library in Dun Laoghaire, in County Dublin, near to where I lived at that time. I went there fairly regularly but on this particular day I was drawn to a section of the library that I had never previously explored. I wasn't looking for anything in particular, but my usual reading material was mainly fiction, occasionally biographies. A book entitled *A World Beyond*, by Ruth Montgomery, an American journalist, seemed to jump out at me. Looking back, I don't think there was anything special about the title or the cover that appealed to me. In any event, I borrowed the book and was fascinated by the scenario of life after death that it presented. Ruth Montgomery had received communication from Arthur Ford, a well-known

American medium until his death in 1971, and in *A World Beyond* she detailed everything that she had learned from him. I was transfixed.

Not long afterwards I happened to see a television programme in which somebody was talking about spirit guides continually connecting with humans. The comforting feelings about guardian angels that I had held as a child, but had latterly submerged, resurfaced. In tandem with the message contained in Ruth Montgomery's book, I could sense that something was at work.

I find it hard to describe what happened next, but suddenly there were voices in my head, talking continually, but with a consciousness that definitely wasn't mine. They weren't talking about the meaning of life or any deep philosophical stuff; it was as if we were having a chat about mundane things, as humans do with each other. What on earth was going on? The voices were there when I woke up in the morning, as I went about my work, as I talked to my wife, Phyllis, and my children, Brian and Aisling, and when I went to bed at night.

Voices in my head? I wondered about my sanity. At times the doubts and fears of my early conditioning came to the surface. Could I be imagining it all? Was it the devil and all his cohorts of evil spirits playing tricks on me?

I wasn't frightened, though, because the voices weren't being malicious. What they were saying wasn't even important or memorable. They were notable only for the fact that I knew for sure they weren't me. They were spirit guides – or guardian angels – and they were communicating with me. They weren't visible to me, except occasionally as light shapes, but I could hear them as clearly as I could any humans, even though there was no sound.

In some ways it was like a 'before and after' situation. All I can say is that before this moment I was living and working conservatively on a day-to-day basis. After, I was outwardly doing the same things, but my inner world was blown apart.

Why was this happening? Would I be better off if I could go back to being the way I was before?

And yet I didn't want to go back – even though I found it very difficult to cope with ordinary, everyday life. I wanted to get away by myself to savour it all, and yet I felt I had to continue with my daily round of family and work responsibilities as if nothing had changed. Strangely, no one seemed to notice anything unusual about me. I didn't want to talk to anyone, including my family, about it. Maybe my acting experience was helpful in that context.

After a few months I realised that I couldn't go on existing in what seemed like a multiplicity of worlds. The voices were too distracting. Since I was on planet earth, I'd either have to leave it or be grounded in the experience of it. Then it came to me that the answer was simple – I could just ask my guides to control what was coming to me, to let it happen only by arrangement. I asked by sending a thought to them and, miraculously, what had been a constant stream of communication stopped immediately. Perversely, I was disappointed, but at least I was able to function more easily within the physical reality of my environment.

That early babble of voices was, I later learned, a sort of concentrated training course to enable me to integrate my communication with my guides with my day-to-day activities. What they were doing was showing me that it was the most ordinary thing in the world to be communicating with each other, and they achieved that objective. One of my guides explained to me that the communication would always be only a thought away, but at my convenience and readiness to receive it.

What was it like? I communicated with my thoughts, not aloud. The best way I can describe it is as a sort of telepathy – I communicated with my guides with my mind and they communicated with me in the same way. I suppose it is much like the silent prayers that some people may send out before bed at night. They don't speak aloud, but are communicating nonetheless.

As far as I was aware, the climate in Ireland in the 1970s and early 1980s did not encourage what might be categorised as paranormal experiences. For that reason, or perhaps because I was excessively sensitive about being considered 'different', 'odd' or in need of psychiatric care, I lived a double life for quite a long time. I had a secret, internal life that I shared with ethereal beings and I managed to combine it with a conventional, external life in which I apparently conformed with the rules of society in the regulation of which I played an official part. All that didn't cause me any stress; in fact, I enjoyed it.

People have often asked me how I became aware of the gift that enabled me to connect with the next world. I never thought of it as a gift as such. In fact, I believed and I still very much believe that it is something that is open to anyone who does not dismiss the possibility. I have attempted to describe the sort of internal revolution that seemed to occur all at once – rather like getting a hole in the head and all sorts of things flowing in. In fact, this may be the most perfect analogy; if people knew about what I was experiencing they may have thought I *had* gone soft in the head. All I can say is that one minute the phenomenon wasn't there, and the next it was.

Word gets around

One evening I was visiting a house where a small group of acquaintances had gathered. The subject of conversation turned to auras. At the time, the idea that all people have auras around them – which show as lights following the outline of their bodies – certainly wasn't familiar to the majority of people with whom I had contact. It was a bit of a risqué belief, and probably pretty controversial. Since then, of course, the existence of auras is, I think, widely accepted – and it has even been demonstrated with a special form of photography known as Kirlian photography, after the Russian technician Demyon D. Kirlian, who developed it in 1939. It wasn't until the 1970s that Kirlian photography hit the US, and most certainly later than that when it was unveiled in Ireland. But it was new and quirky, and somebody in our group got the idea that we should try looking at each others' auras.

Auras can probably be best described as energy fields that surround our bodies – sort of radiate out from them. We all have them, but the question was, that evening, could we see them? We felt that we'd have the best chance of succeeding if each person in turn sat against a white background. The rest of us would concentrate on looking (in as relaxed a way as we could) at and around that person. Some of my acquaintances quickly saw a light around the person – either white, or in colour. I didn't see anything at all, but I suddenly started getting all sorts of impressions about the person sitting down: about her relationship with her partner, her feelings about her career, the place where she lived. I passed them on and she said that they were not only very relevant, but helpful for what was happening in her life at that time. The impressions didn't come to me visually or as if somebody was soundlessly putting words into my mouth; they simply dropped into my mind and I articulated them as clearly as I could in my own words.

After that, the other guests asked me to do the same thing for them, with similar results. At this remove, all I can remember is that the general reaction was one of surprise and interest – which, I suppose, would have been true for me as well. It was all very odd.

As I didn't want to be put into any sort of 'guru' slot, I asked the group to keep quiet about what had happened. Since the spirit guides first made themselves known to me, I've made every attempt to avoid putting myself into the limelight, and I continue to do so to this day. These are private conversations, and while I am always more than happy to use the information they provide to help others, it would be all too easy to become a sort of modern-day medium, and have my life taken over. I invariably aimed to forget whatever transpired in my individual sessions with people in case I might, unconsciously, reveal something that they trusted would be confidential.

Slowly but surely the wall that I had tried to build around my secret life began to crumble. Sometimes, much to my embarrassment, and after a little too much to drink, I was a bit too eager to impart the information provided by the spirit guides. As a result, word began to spread and a rapidly increasing number of people began to ask if they could come to see me. I was still very careful not to let any of that impinge on my work life, and kept things quiet when I was with my colleagues. My personal and social life was, however, beginning to follow a new track. The contact with people who were searching for meaning and direction in their lives was like an affirmation for me. I had to accept that guidance was coming to me from some benevolent source or sources outside of myself that I understood to be my guides.

My ability to provide people with guidance continued to perplex me. I had never regarded myself as being abnormally perceptive and, yet, when I asked for guidance I was able to tell people many things about themselves, their past experiences, their families, their relationships, their careers, their challenges and their gifts – facts that I couldn't possibly have known in any other way. Many of these people were strangers to me, and the information I received about them was startlingly vivid and accurate. I was still, at that point, unsure where it was all coming from. I considered all the obvious explanations, such as telepathy, and subconscious or unconscious suggestion, but they made no sense in my situation. If I were using paranormal skills I would have been able to do so all of the time – not just on isolated occasions when people came to me for guidance. I considered it vitally important that I was completely unable to intrude on anyone's privacy unless I was asked to do so by the person concerned.

The trouble was that word was getting around too fast. I was in a senior management position in the Civil Service, and part of my job included implementing a major reorganisation programme to do with property registration. I loved my job. It was enjoyable and fulfilling, but it made a lot of demands on my time. On the domestic front, the telephone was ringing constantly – day and night – with consequential inconvenience for the whole household, as people who had heard of my ability to make contact with spirit guides sought advice. All of this happened entirely through word of mouth. I struggled with my double life until I was given the opportunity to take early retirement from the Civil Service in 1988. This was a turning point for me. I was torn between continuing to do a job I enjoyed and accepting that something much bigger was going on. It was time to do something different with my life.

My family were supportive of my decision to retire from my job. My wife had long been interested in the area of communication with guides. I think they were glad that I was now able to deal with the telephone calls myself because they were less inconvenienced by its demands! And, of course, I was in a position to respond more frequently to requests from people to come to see me. After a session with me, individuals would tell their friends about the results and I'd get more calls until the whole thing snowballed.

Since that time, and across many years, I have had the privilege of meeting thousands of people. I have written eleven books under the pen-name Patrick Francis in collaboration with three spirit beings with whom I have established a strong communication. The first was an ex-nun called Margaret Anna Cusack. The second was Shebaka, an Egyptian pharaoh after whom the Shabaka stone in the British Museum is named. This stone was given to the museum by the First Lord of the

Admiralty, George John, 2nd Earl Spencer (an ancestor of Princess Diana) in 1805, and registered with the museum on 13 July of that year. I spelled Shebaka's name with an 'e' rather than an 'a' because I knew nothing about him initially, so it was a huge surprise when I found out about the stone. The third guide is Jiddhu Krishnamurti, the famous Indian philosopher and teacher. I set up my own self-publishing company but I did not actively seek publicity, nor did I advertise. I believed that people who would be interested in – or benefit from – the material in my books would be drawn to them. That arrangement suited me and it worked well.

One of the most rewarding and compellingly enlightening elements of my new work involved individual sessions with people. During these sessions all sorts of issues surfaced, including wide-ranging fears, relationship difficulties, career problems, a search for meaning in life, depression, financial issues, guilt, past lives, the desire for contact with 'dead' loved ones, communication with spirit guides, health problems, curiosity about what happens after the death of the body, and more. Most of these issues fell outside my own range of experience, which helped me to be non-judgemental in my approach. People came to see me about anything and everything, and the sessions that ensued moved into areas that were not confined to the particular issue that troubled my visitors. The floodgates were opened during our sessions, and both my visitors and I were often dumbstruck by what evolved.

I remained reluctant to intrude on people's privacy unless they were completely open to the idea of hearing what the guides had to say. I knew nothing about the vast majority of my visitors, and put complete trust in my spirit guides to supply insights that would be in their best interests.

My life had changed, and through that I was beginning to help to change the lives of others. My story doesn't stop here, though; in fact, this is and was just the beginning. I continued to devote a good proportion of my life to providing the guidance that the spirit guides offered. Later on in the book I will be going into more detail about guides and making suggestions about how people can connect with their own guides, if they so wish. First, though, since the book is primarily about what happens to people when they die, I must introduce the soul who inspired this book and who, as Margaret Anna Cusack, lived on earth from 1829 to 1899.

Chapter 2

Meeting Margaret Anna

In the late 1970s, shortly before I was, or more accurately agreed to be, catapulted into my new double life, I had an idea to try and write a film script about Daniel O'Connell, a charismatic Irish historical figure. He was a renowned barrister, the first Catholic member of the House of Commons in 1828 and the main campaigner for Catholic emancipation, which included the right of Catholics and Presbyterians and members of all Christian faiths (other than the established Church of England, which already had the exclusive right) to sit in Parliament. The enabling law was passed in 1829.

While I was researching O'Connell's life I was guided to a rare biography of him, written by M.F. Cusack. In much the same way as I had been guided to Ruth Montgomery's book in the library in Dun Laoghaire, I found myself holding the biography in my hands without consciously having sought it. I later discovered that the author was a woman usually known as Margaret Anna Cusack.

Something very odd happened when I held that book in my hands for the first time. I heard, or at least sensed, a new voice. Like the other guides who had entered my life, Margaret Anna introduced herself by way of a sort of telepathic communication. I looked down and saw her name, and there she was communicating with me. I was astonished to discover that this new voice belonged to someone who had been 'real'. It hadn't ever occurred to me that the guardian angels or spirit guides had been people who lived on earth. Up to that point I thought of them as ethereal beings. Why was this woman contacting me? Where did she come from? I had to find out.

Margaret Anna was a nineteenth-century celebrity; through her writing and her campaign for social reform she had become internationally famous as the 'Nun of Kenmare'. Born in Dublin in 1829, she was brought up as a member of the Anglican Church. In her teens her parents separated and she moved to England with her mother. In due course she became engaged to a young man called Charles Holmes; however, during a visit to Ireland to see her father, who was very ill, she got news that Charles had died suddenly. She was devastated. She wrote : '*I lay in a darkened room for months for it seemed to me as if the sunlight was too glad.*'

After a period of mourning, Margaret Anna turned to intensive religious searching that led to her becoming an Anglican nun. About five years later, in 1859, she converted to Roman Catholicism, and a year after that she entered a Poor Clare convent in Newry, County Down, in Ireland. There she took the name Sister M. Francis Clare.

In 1861 Margaret Anna moved to Kenmare in County Kerry to help found a branch of her order there. She wrote prolifically and her books had wide international circulation, with the proceeds going to support the Poor Clares and their work with the poor. In total she published more than fifty books, including *A Student's History of Ireland*, *Woman's Work in Modern Society*, biographies of St Patrick, St Columba and St Bridget, and two autobiographies, *The Nun of Kenmare* and *The Story of My Life*. Her novels include *Ned Rusheen, or Who Fired the First Shot?*, and *Tim O'Halloran's Choice*. She also wrote songs, music and verse, and founded Kenmare Publications, through which 200,000 volumes of her works were issued in under ten years. She kept two full-time secretaries occupied, publicly railed against landlords, and wrote letters on Irish causes to the Irish, American and Canadian press.

Quite simply, Margaret Anna was a feisty, driven and strong-minded character, with a raft of interests and a dogged determination to make a difference. She railed against social injustice, and actively sought political and social reform. She drew attention to the needs of the underprivileged, and fought for equal rights for women. She was passionate about education, and is reputed to have been instrumental in saving thousands of people from dying of starvation when she founded a Famine Relief Fund in 1879. Most astonishingly, she attained this high public profile from within a cloistered institution.

With her passionate enthusiasm and impatience for creating a just social order she came to be seen as a thorn in the sides of her ecclesiastical superiors. Having incurred the disapproval of the Bishop of Kerry she left Kenmare in 1881. It would be naïve to expect that a nun with such an internationally public profile as a social agitator would earn the approval of the hierarchy. They expected nuns to get on with their lives and work quietly and obediently, without seeking to upset the established order of things, as Margaret Anna was doing. In the nineteenth century women were still generally treated as second-class citizens – mere chattels in the eyes of the law.

Despite her brave attempts to elicit change, Margaret Anna was poorly treated by the Irish church hierarchy. On one occasion she paid a visit to the Convent of the Poor Clares, in Harold's Cross, Dublin, *en route* to Newry. Here she was warmly welcomed by the nuns and arranged to return to the convent soon after. However, before her scheduled return the Archbishop of Dublin, Cardinal McCabe, visited the convent and ordered the nuns not to allow her to stay there that night. She was left to find alternative accommodation – quite shocking treatment considering the fact that she had been experiencing heart problems.

Margaret Anna was not inclined to give up easily, however, and over the following two years she sought to implement her plans to help the underprivileged in Ireland. It was a tiring and thankless task. Exhausted by the continuing struggle, she moved to Nottingham in England in 1883. With the approval and support of Bishop Bagshawe of Nottingham and authorisation from Pope Leo XXIII, she founded the Order of Sisters of St Joseph of Peace early in 1884. The goals of the Order were to choose works for peace that would especially benefit the poor.

Due to lack of funds, the fledgling Order was curtailed in the progress of its mission. Conscious that Margaret Anna was well known in America (as the 'Nun of Kenmare'), Bishop Bagshawe asked her to go there to seek help. In spite of medical advice that she was unfit for such a long journey because of her heart condition, she set sail for America late in 1884.

To her utter surprise and disappointment, she was met with a blank wall of non-cooperation by the hierarchy in New York. Her reputation as the Nun of Kenmare, an internationally renowned author and social reformer, had preceded her. Put simply, she was regarded as a troublemaker to be ignored.

One man, however, was willing to stand up for her. Bishop Wigger of Newark realised the value of her work and invited her to his diocese. In March 1886 she established a branch of her Order in New Jersey. But the hierarchical grapevine conspired against her in her efforts to expand the work of the Order throughout America. It didn't help that so many of the American hierarchy were of Irish extraction and aware of the Irish church authorities' opinions about her. Deeply anguished, in 1888 she decided that the work of the Order would not prosper while she was connected with it, and she resigned.

Having formally left her position as Mother General of the Order, her personal integrity wouldn't allow her to remain as a member of a Church with such inflexible patriarchal structures, and to a large extent she reverted to the Anglican beliefs of her early life. She was in much demand as a lecturer and travelled widely throughout America speaking to large audiences.

At the end of 1891 Margaret Anna returned to England, where, despite increasingly failing health, she continued to write. She died in Leamington, England, on 5 June 1899. Her name was excised as the founder of her Order because she was branded as an apostate by the Catholic Church. It was not restored until 1970.

Margaret Anna was a remarkable, pioneering woman, and in her evolved spirit state she continues to be a source of inspiration and help to all those in need. I know her intimately now, and she comes across as a warm, humorous and completely non-pious woman – always direct, and endearingly honest. Above all, she emphatically conveys what an exhilarating experience life – continuing life – can be. I knew that before she died she was in a debilitated physical condition. Yet here she was – very much alive in another form, and showing in a most vivid and exciting way that life is a continuing adventure.

In my experience, one of the peculiarities of being human is that we like freedom, but (somewhat contradictorily) we also like being told what to do. We want guidance to follow our own path. Some people might consider guardian angels – spirit guides – as benign dictators who plot the course of our lives and tell us how to live them. This couldn't be more wrong, as I soon discovered.

In the spirit world free will is sacrosanct, and at an evolved level of awareness there can never be interference with it. So when I refer to being in constant communication with Margaret Anna, I mean that the communication is unobtrusive and doesn't impinge in any obvious way on my day-to-day life. When I feel I need help, I ask for it through my thoughts. I trust that it will come, and it does – often in a manner that I would never have anticipated.

In 1998 I was looking through some papers when a news-paper feature about Margaret Anna from a decade earlier liter-ally jumped out at me. I'd put it to one side years ago, and completely forgotten about it. Here it was again, and I knew there was a message for me. As I looked at it I received a strong message that Margaret Anna wanted to collaborate with me in writing a book. After a lapse of over twenty years since our initial contact I was surprised, but delighted, by that develop-ment. By that stage I knew not to ask what the book would be about. I trusted that that would be revealed in due course.

Margaret Anna Cusack was a remarkable woman by any stan-dards. In having the honour of collaborating with her I'm expressing my admiration and respect for her as an outstanding pioneering spirit to whom the world owes much. Later on in the book she describes how, after her passing, she reviewed what she had achieved while she was on earth – an assessment of her earthly life.

In her life on earth Margaret Anna presented us with an inspirational example of the significant, even though often unacknowledged, impact one person can make on global consciousness. And she's obviously not resting on her laurels. So many of us play down our potential, and believe that one person cannot make a real difference. Margaret Anna has shown otherwise, and one of the most important elements of this book is based on her wish that people live their lives to the fullest, and make the most of what they have. The overriding message of this book is one of hope. Margaret Anna's wish is that all souls will be released from victimhood – particularly that of fear – so that all can experience their blissful heritage of unconditional love.

My introduction to Margaret Anna and my continuing relationship with her were hugely influential factors in my fuller involvement in the lives of others – giving 'readings' to individuals and later writing books, running courses and doing talks. I just accept that she's there and I ask for her help as I feel I need it. As will be obvious from later chapters in this book, she's involved in all sorts of helpful activities and I'm only one of her many 'charges'.

Chapter 3

Life after Death

My journey through life has confirmed my acceptance of the continuity of life after death. I grew up believing that we were confined to a specific fate according to our behaviour on earth, but what I learned next made much more sense to me. There was no fear in this new understanding; it soon became clear that life after death not only existed, but was a vibrant, positive experience. I'd always been open to (and found great comfort in) the idea that I had guardian angels helping me through life. They continue to do so, and through them I am able to help others as well.

Margaret Anna is just one of those guardian angels who has changed my life forever. The fact that she was a real person, who actually existed in the 'real world' before her death in 1899, undoubtedly provided proof of the continuity of life. She is now sharing her wisdom with humans on earth, and I have no doubts about her existence. But life in spirit is something very different from life on earth, and Margaret Anna has been hugely influential in defining and explaining that world. I can't hop in and out of the spirit world in order to carry back shoals of information. Fortunately, there are evolved and generous souls like Margaret Anna who want to lift the burden of fear from us by telling us what to expect when the time comes for us to move on. Through Margaret Anna and to a lesser extent my other guides I have learned a great deal about the 'next life'.

By the time I came to write this book I had been used to the idea of Margaret Anna as one of my spirit guides for many years and I certainly wasn't slow in asking for her help when I found myself, as I often did, in challenging situations. I didn't bother waiting for answers. I just asked and trusted that the answers would come in their own good time, which they invariably did.

Collaborating with Margaret Anna on a book was a different, perhaps more immediate, type of experience. My communication with her wasn't like having an ordinary conversation with another human being. She didn't come and sit beside me and I didn't see her or visualise her. (Later on I saw photographs of her in her older age, but at first I had no idea what she looked like.) The only way I can describe the communication is that I felt her presence – a warm, comforting, humorous sort of feeling – so I knew when the communication was happening and when it wasn't. She wasn't using words but, rather, conveying impressions to me that I expressed in my own words. It was a seamless type of experience that, I suppose, could be regarded as similar to telepathy, although that's an inadequate description. Even though it would have been easier for me if I could have just written down words coming directly from her, it was more fulfilling for me to use my own words – and, of course, that helped me to raise my level of consciousness.

I was also reassured by the fact that she wouldn't let me get away with any misinterpretations. How did I know this? I just did, in the same way that I knew when she was communicating with me and when she wasn't. In our first session Margaret Anna conveyed that she'd like to talk about her own experience since she passed on. I could hardly wait to hear more about that. I don't think it's an exaggeration to say that what happens after the death of the body is a 'burning' question; certainly it is for the people I have met over many years. I suggest that even the 'when you're dead, you're dead' brigade have some niggles of curiosity about it from time to time.

I personally didn't have any doubts about the continuity of life. I never kept any records of my individual sessions with people, as it was vitally important for them that they could trust in the confidentiality of whatever transpired at our meetings, but occasionally something memorable emerged, which stayed in my mind. I didn't have any particular agenda when people came to me; obviously, spontaneity was an essential ingredient in the whole process.

I preferred to concentrate on communication with guides, and to address career or relationship issues – or generally philosophical matters. But my meetings were always different, and the tone and the content were guided by the needs of my visitors, and the communication with the guides. In the early stages I actively hoped that messages from 'dead' relatives didn't come through, mainly because I didn't want to risk misleading anyone. I wanted to be absolutely sure that whatever connection I made in such a sensitive area was 100 per cent genuine. I suppose also that I didn't fully trust my ability as a communicator. But some readings undoubtedly had a mediumistic element – where the communication was coming from a relative or friend of the person seeking the reading. The readings took place in an intimate setting (a small room) devoid of any distractions, the main feature being two comfortable chairs – one for myself and the other for the sitter. The duration of the readings was approximately two hours. What happened within those two hours was largely beyond my control.

Working with my guides was altogether different from trying to connect with somebody who might be totally new to that type of communication. But, as time went on, and almost in spite of myself, I got messages and information for many people from relatives or friends who had passed on. The nature of the information was such that there could be no doubt about the authenticity of the experiences. Sometimes what I was receiving from my contacts in spirit made no sense to me, but when I plucked up the courage to convey it to the people concerned it was invariably significant for them.

Two sessions in particular spring to mind. I have altered the names of the sitters to protect their identity. I don't like the word 'medium' but, as I can't think of a better alternative to convey the sense of a bridge between the physical and the spirit worlds, it will have to do.

Becoming a medium

One day, many years ago, I had an appointment with a woman called Josephine. While I was waiting for her at my home, a man's name kept repeating over and over in my head. This was unusual for me, as I never asked for or received any advance information before a meeting. When Josephine arrived, I mentioned the name to her and she reacted instantly. The name I had heard was that of her husband, who had died many years previously. Immediately I felt him coming through to me, telling me that he had died while he was tying his shoelaces. I know 'coming through' is a strange sort of expression to use, but I think it's a more accurate way of saying that I felt him 'telling' me, as we weren't actually 'talking' as such.

I hesitated about saying this to Josephine, because it sounded so strange, but the voice was insistent, and so I said it.

'Oh, yes,' she said very matter-of-factly. 'He was out in the yard bending down to tie his shoelaces when a tractor backed into him and killed him.'

After that there was no stopping him; he gave her all sorts of information and advice about various personal and business matters. At this stage I have no recollection of what they were; in any case, they would only have been of interest to her. I remember, though, how delighted I was by the session with her. She was obviously very pleased about the contact with her late husband.

A few months later I met a woman named Anne. Once again I was visited by a communicator, who absolutely insisted that I pass on a message. The message or, more accurately, the instruction, was: '*Tell her to play a piece of string.*'

This seemed completely nonsensical to me. I was thinking of 'string' being a slender rope of some kind. However, when I eventually took a chance and told her, Anne lit up immediately. The spirit was a friend of Anne's, and she had been wondering what music to play at a memorial service for him. She knew exactly what he meant – music played by string instruments. She didn't seem to be surprised – but I was.

These and other experiences have provided me with plenty of incontrovertible evidence of continuing life. My communication with Margaret Anna has, therefore, always made sense to me, and I've never doubted that the details she has provided about the spirit world are accurate and believable. In many of the experiences I had provided information that sounded superficial to me, but was deeply moving or important to the people receiving the messages. However, the very fact that it was possible for both sides of the physical and spirit dimensions to make contact was comforting, particularly because it was obviously genuine. I was eager for more information – and a wider discussion of life in general in the spirit dimension – and that's where Margaret Anna came in.

Living after death

Like many others, I was often wrenched by agonising self-questioning. In most of my communications, when people came to see me, I had proof that the communication was accurate because it was confirmed. In Margaret Anna's case I was working in the dark. Was I fooling myself into thinking that the soul who was Margaret Anna Cusack was *actually* communicating with me? And by questioning this communication, was I showing a lack of trust? Margaret Anna had been such a celebrity in her earthly life, I wondered if I had just somehow extrapolated information about her and created artificial communications. I was worried, too, that the information I was transcribing might in some way create a misleading impression about her.

Margaret Anna gave short shrift to my qualms. She suggested that we forget about all that and get on with the project that would become this book. She began by describing to me her own death: *'My friends put on my coffin: "Margaret Anna Cusack fell asleep June 5th, 1899, aged 70 years." The thought was nice. I said goodbye to my poor old body, which had been tired out for a long time. It had struggled with ill-health for many years and had lasted a lot longer than I could reasonably have expected.'*

Margaret Anna looked on as her friends lovingly dealt with her body. After the burial ceremonies were over, she suddenly became aware of what she could only describe as a radiant being smiling at her and then giving her a big hug. Without any perception of movement she found herself as a guest of honour at a big welcoming party. It was a wonderfully joyful reunion with many friends.

I asked her whatever questions occurred to me and she answered them directly, without any evasion. Did she expect to be judged after her arrival? She did, she said, but there wasn't any sign of anything like that.

How did she recognise her friends? She said she just knew them. They were like effulgent beings of light, yet easily distinguishable one from another.

Were there gender distinctions in spirit? She answered: *'There were and there weren't. I know that's a strange kind of answer. The best way I can try to explain it is that there was a transcendence of gender, like, say, when you communicate on a soul level with somebody. Yet there were some whom I had known as female and some as male, and I seemed to communicate with them in that way and they with me.'*

Was there any sexual frisson? *'I wasn't always a nun! Yes, there was sexual frisson, as you put it, in the sense of a wonderful joyful intimacy, which is what sexuality involves, as I understand it.'*

In asking her questions, I was aware that I was thinking in a linear way, from a time and space point of view. In her new situation it seemed as if everything was happening simultaneously. She explained that she was no longer aware of time. She was still getting used to feeling completely free. On earth she was always busy – things to be done, ideas to be explored, books to be written, bishops to be cajoled. Now here she was with no agenda, but full of the joy of just being, and surrounded by kindred spirits in every sense of the word.

In order to help me understand, she explained that the reunion went on for maybe a few hours or maybe a few days in my time. She hadn't yet completely shaken off the feelings of illness and tiredness that were her constant companions on earth. At some stage one of her old/new friends suggested that she might like to take a little rest. She agreed, and instantly she seemed to be lying on a wonderfully comfortable bed in a beautifully appointed room with soft music enveloping her. She relaxed into the harmony of it all. She said that it was misleading to talk of things happening in sequence, because everything seemed to be happening all at once.

In any event, the relaxation process refreshed her and, once again, she found herself with a group of the friends she had met earlier. They had a lot of catching up to do. I asked her whether she was beginning to be curious about what she was going to be doing. I said that I couldn't imagine her being happy sitting around relaxing and doing nothing, no matter how enjoyable the company.

She replied that she didn't have to do anything – but that she wasn't doing 'nothing'. Impressions were coming to her all the time. Even as she thought about something – for example, how her Sisters from the Order were getting on – she found she was able to get a picture or a vision of that immediately. It was all completely effortless. She asked me to imagine this scenario: I want to visit my friends in America. I have to go through a lengthy process of booking tickets, paying fares, hours of travel interspersed with delays at airports. But in the world she was now in, there was none of that. The only drawback was that she couldn't converse with her sisters in the Order or touch them. She could talk to them, but they didn't hear her. Initially, that was a big disappointment, particularly as she had had to suffer the pain of separation from them while she was bodily on earth. After a while she adjusted to the way things were and began to enjoy helping out in unobtrusive ways.

Who is God?

Early on in our communication I asked Margaret Anna whether it was possible to prove for those of us on earth that there is life after death. *'It's often said that there is no proof of life after death, because no one ever comes back to tell their relatives, friends or even interested researchers about their new life; however, this is not the case. Many souls have been communicating through the centuries with those humans who have been open to receiving them so I can't take any credit in projecting, as it were, a voice from the grave.'*

Margaret Anna was very easy to work with, and her sense of humour was always evident in all of our communications. She regularly teased me, for example, by saying she knew that I had thought she looked very grim in the photographs I had seen of her, and we developed a light-hearted sort of banter that belied the extraordinary level and content of the information she passed on to me. It was strange for me getting used to the idea that she could read my thoughts like that, but as our conversations continued I got used to it.

My main goal in our early communications was to ask exactly what happens when our body 'dies' and we pass over.

Margaret Anna said that she experienced a lot of confusion in the aftermath of her passing. She had changed religions, had been a social reformer, had been regarded as a nuisance by her ecclesiastical superiors, and she had been vilified and condemned as an apostate. As she says, *'It seemed as if I had created conflict where I had wanted harmony, and hate where I wanted love.'*

She had become so accustomed to rejection, she was very concerned about what God would be like. What if He turned out to be like the figures of authority that she had known in the past?

I assumed that, as Margaret Anna Cusack, and then perhaps more particularly as Sister/Mother Francis Clare, she would have built up a relationship with God as a Supreme Being in some form. I asked her where God fitted into her new situation. She replied, *'For a start, there was still no sign of any call to judgment and I began to realise that there wouldn't be. There wasn't any indication of God wanting to see me for any other reason either, which was both a relief and a disappointment.'*

In my interaction with spirit beings I needed to be completely relaxed and quiet in my mind. I had an arrangement with Margaret Anna that whenever I felt tired or unclear we discontinued our sessions.

When I indicated to her that I was ready to continue, she said: *'I was releasing the mental restrictions that were built up in my physical lifetime – having, of course, already released the material ones. Impressions came flooding back to me of what I had previously known, including the notion of God, not as a separate being, but as the life force in all of us. There was to be no judgment other than that which I chose to make on myself.'*

While I was writing down these words, I recalled an occasion when I was travelling on a bus one evening. I was in a sort of meditative mood and I hoped that nobody would sit beside me and start talking to me. There seemed to be a good chance I'd be left in peace as there was a number of empty seats on the bus. Even so, a woman got on the bus and made a beeline for the seat beside me. I can't describe her very well, as I was trying not to look at her, but I could see out of the corner of my eye that she was a large lady, conservatively dressed. She sat down firmly and decisively, with a very strong physical presence. I kept my eyes closed, pretending to be dozing, but that didn't work.

She said in a loud voice: 'They're real places, you know.'

I mumbled something, not wanting to encourage her by asking the obvious question. That didn't stop her. She repeated her statement, so I felt I had to ask what places she was talking about.

'Heaven, Hell and Purgatory,' she answered.

I didn't make any comment, but she went on to tell me that a woman in Austria had seen them in a vision and was able to describe the suffering in Purgatory and Hell in gruesome detail.

Eventually I could keep quiet no longer. I said, 'There aren't any such places. They're all states of mind.'

That led to a verbal deluge about how wrong I was. Then, with a triumphant flourish, she stood up and said, 'You'll find out soon enough.'

She left the bus – and me to my fate!

So what was the truth? The Heaven, Hell and Purgatory scenario most certainly wasn't like anything Margaret Anna had described. And what about God? Where did he fit in?

A loving union

The God of my youth was a patriarchal figure with a long white beard and a rather frightening expression – or so I thought. It wasn't difficult to imagine Him (always a capital 'H') doling out severe punishment for even minor transgressions. It's understandable that I thought that way – we are all conditioned to impose a sort of structure on concepts, so that we can relate them to our own experience. So, in order to understand something, we tend to put onto it a form that's familiar to us. This does, however, have the unfortunate effect of imposing limits on our thinking.

The same can be applied to the notion of God, to whom we give a 'form' that we can understand. It followed that God had to be a 'person', albeit one who could see, hear and know everything going on in the world – and be everywhere, all at the same time. His ability to achieve all of this had to be taken on trust; it would only be possible to accept His existence and His role if we believed.

As far as I'm aware, most, if not all, religious teaching focuses on the idea of separateness; in other words, there's a Supreme Being (God) who created all souls and is separate from them. Because God is separate, He has the ultimate prerogative of sitting in judgment on us. Interestingly, however, every one of my spirit guides stresses that the idea of separateness is what delays the evolution of life on earth in terms of awareness. They

38

are adamant that whatever we call the animating force of life – God, the Universe or unconditional love – is not separate from us but that we are all part of it.

In order to understand that concept, we need to dispense with any notions of form or structure. I like to use the description 'unconditional love' because it makes it impossible for me to fall into a trap of trying to fit that into any kind of structure. While I can't fully understand how it all works, I find it easy to accept its infinite, unlimited nature, as I don't see how it can be enclosed within any boundaries, not even beginnings and endings.

Margaret Anna and all those souls who act as our guides are helping us to free ourselves from the feeling of separateness, and to align ourselves with unconditional love. In that way we're no longer in a 'Him' and 'us' situation but, rather, in a loving union with the source of all life. A simple (but ultimately inadequate) analogy is that of a drop of water being in the ocean but the ocean also being in the drop of water. In other words, there's no separation between the drop of water and the ocean. Extending the analogy to ourselves we can understand and, ideally, accept that we, however limited and insignificant we may perceive ourselves to be, are part of that unconditional, infinite, loving energy and can allow ourselves to be supported by its unlimited power.

Another analogy was suggested to me by Jiddhu Krishnamurti (whose stated mission in his earthly life was to set people absolutely, unconditionally, free from all forms of conditioning). Suppose we say that there's an everlasting light in each person. There's an equivalent potential brightness in each light. In some people it shines dimly, in others it's glowing a little brighter, in still others the glow is stronger; in each one the glow is at a different level of brightness. What switches the light to an increasing level of brightness is the quality of the inner life of each person – security, self-esteem, an ability to respond spontaneously to the flow of light, and, above all, freedom from rigidity of thinking, going within, and allowing the light to spread throughout the whole being. As each light glows ever more brightly, it connects with all the other lights and illuminates the whole universe.

The universal connection might perhaps be illustrated by representing each person as a perpetually lighting candle with its own distinctive colour. The light from each candle spreads into a huge glow throughout the universe. Yet each candle retains its individuality, while being part of the whole confluence of light.

So it is that each soul is a part of God and God is in each soul.

Margaret Anna had explained to me that each of us is a soul in spirit before we are born into our physical lives, and I asked her why she didn't carry the concept of God that she had known at that time into her life as a nun.

She explained that her aim in that life was to be an agent of change, a reformer, and that it was necessary for her to go into an environment and to be part of it before she could seek to transform it. She had to have a passion for what she was doing. She couldn't be an outsider. Where there was injustice, she needed to be a victim of it. Where there was sadness, grief and loneliness, she needed to experience them. She needed to be human in every sense of what that meant at that stage of human evolution. She also needed to be female, because human evolution would remain stagnant unless it could be rescued by a balancing of male and female consciousness within individuals and then globally.

In the context of the nineteenth century, her priority was to try to create a climate of improved conditions for people, particularly those who had unequal rights and opportunities, such as women and the poor who, of course, included both sexes.

She said to me, *'I felt that my role was to be a launching pad from which others could orbit. I sought to be a pragmatist rather than a philosopher – or perhaps, to be a pragmatic philosopher! Perceptions of God could wait. In any case, they would be as individual as souls and would continue to be. We could explore the higher reaches of spiritual expression when people were more comfortable in their living conditions as well as their self-esteem.'*

The concept of God that Margaret Anna outlined wasn't new to me, as it had been conveyed by Shebaka to me in previous communications. I accepted it completely as the only philosophy that made sense of life to me.

As she had promised, Margaret Anna had chosen to begin the process of illustrating what happens after the death of the body by outlining her own experience, including her apprehension about whether or how she might be judged, and where God fitted into the whole picture of life after death. Her constant rejection during her life on earth by the ecclesiastical authorities hadn't helped to set her mind at ease on those questions. The answers she discovered (or rediscovered, I should say) and outlined are clear and unambiguous.

I found her way of unfolding the evolution of her experience most illuminating and comforting. Already she had shown that there was nothing to fear about the experience of death.

Chapter 4

In Come the Guides

In the early years after I found I could communicate with spirit guides, my main contact was with Shebaka. I wrote my first books about what he communicated to me. But by the time I started work on this book, Margaret Anna was the main spirit with whom I had regular 'conversations', although I still got interjections from others from time to time.

Margaret Anna seemed as keen as I was to explore the details of life after our death on earth, and to tell me all about her personal experience of settling in to a new life in spirit. She wanted me to pass on this information to others here on earth so that they know what to expect.

'I want to shout a big YES to life, to the death of death, if I might put it like that, so that anybody and everybody can say, "I know my body is going to die, but I know, too, that there's nothing to fear in that – it's a celebration of continuing transformation in life." I want to go into details about

how I express myself in my present state and what life in
spirit generally is like.'

She answered question after question, explaining the intricacies of the process of death, as I tried to make sense of it all. Her answers jumped around like a patchwork that I had to make sense of. Sometimes she moved on from a topic and came back to it later, when she knew I was ready to hear about it. I never knew where our communications would lead, but I was heartened by everything I found out.

I discovered, for example, that it's usual to have a looking-back process or 'review' of the physical life that is over. That's when we assess how well we succeeded in whatever we set out to achieve in our lives. Of course, we may find ourselves disappointed by our efforts. It's not intended to be a guilt-inducing exercise but, rather, an objective look at our progress on earth. Margaret Anna emphasised the fact that there is no pressure; we judge ourselves when we feel ready to do so. In fact, no one forces us to do anything at all, which would be interfering with our free will.

Although a review can be a positive experience, I did wonder if people might be anxious about looking back on past performance. Certainly it's a far cry from presenting ourselves for judgment, as is often traditionally taught, but nonetheless it can be a daunting prospect. Margaret Anna's experience was bound to be helpful, so I asked her whether she felt that she had achieved what she set out to achieve when she looked back at her earthly life.

She answered that, on the whole, she did. In her later years on earth she didn't experience much of a sense of achievement. She had written a lot and talked a lot; she had raised a considerable amount of money to help people in need. She had consistently served in as loving a way as she could. But she had also been a source of dissent, and many of her projects had collapsed. She was often disillusioned and she see-sawed between religions. At the end, very much alone apart from a few stalwart friends, she couldn't see herself as anything other than a failure, well-intentioned though she was. But, she told me:

'In spirit there was – there always is – a very different perspective. It's a futile and altogether pointless exercise trying to judge a life's expression within its time span. When I looked at that earth life from the much broader vantage point of spirit I saw that, through my writings, my talks, my contacts with people, the ideas I put into motion, my passion for equal opportunities for everybody, I had opened doors to the raising of consciousness outside of the limits of a particular time scale. In other words, I had made a contribution – the effects of which would live on after I passed on. Once I had taken that on board in spirit I was able to forgive myself for all the human failings I had manifested and let myself enjoy the freedom I now had.'

Love after death

One of the major tragedies in our lives is when we lose our loved ones. I have come across this sort of situation many times and it can be heartbreakingly sad. Margaret Anna mentioned how much in love she had been with her fiancé Charles Holmes, her devastation when he died, and how different her future life would have been had he lived. But the good news is that they have resumed their relationship. She says, *'We love each other in a more complete way than would have been possible on earth.'*

So, while the pain of physical separation is very hard to bear there is great comfort in the thought that we will not only see our loved ones again, but also resume our relationships with them in a more profound way. Anything that is possible on earth is possible in spirit.

Communicating with guides

As I mentioned earlier, as a child I found great comfort in the idea of guardian angels, who were always helping me in a loving way. There was no fear associated with them. They helped me in ways too numerous to mention, and my belief that they were there, by my side, protecting me and my family from whatever I believed might endanger us, made my childhood infinitely calmer.

As I grew up into adulthood, I continued to believe in guardian angels – long after I had discounted most of the other elements of the belief systems of my youth. It was not something I actively thought about; rather, they were constantly there, on the periphery of my thoughts, and very real in many senses. In fact, I didn't dwell on the angels much until I was dramatically reminded of their existence later in life. The most significant outcome of what I might call my reawakening was my acceptance not just of the reality of guardian angels, but the fact that it was possible to have conscious communication with them. Perhaps it was my earlier, unconscious acceptance of their existence that made me believe entirely that the voices I was hearing were those of spirits; it was, however, a mind-blowing experience to discover that I could interact with them – and they with me. For many months I experienced a mixture of exhilaration and confusion, until it all settled down. Once I was able to keep the voices at bay until I needed assistance, the relationship became peaceful and utterly comforting.

More than anything I want people to understand my own experience of working with guides, so that they can benefit in the same way. I had a significant process of adaptation in adjusting to the spontaneous way of spirit, which contrasted with the structured physical way we normally operate.

I wondered if guardian angels and spirit guides are the same, or are they distinct entities? Throughout the ages, angels have been pictured wearing wings, which, as a child, I found to be a comforting, sheltering image. I presumed the wings were meant to represent the traditional role ascribed to angels as messengers of God, the means by which they flew around delivering the messages. I like the quotation from G.K. Chesterton which says: 'Angels can fly because they take themselves lightly.' I now know that they do; this is something we all need to do. We can only truly soar when we are light enough to do so.

My understanding, in accordance with the information I have been given by my spirit guides, is that we are all soul – part of God, or 'unconditional love'. In that sense there can be no distinction between angels and guides. Although I prefer the description 'guardian angels' myself, I got into the habit of using the word 'guides', partly because it was shorter but mainly because it had no obvious religious connotation. Anyway, I couldn't imagine Margaret Anna flying around with wings attached to her! The word 'guide' is fitting, too, as their role in our lives is to guide us through both our darkest and our brightest days.

Way back in the 1960s, I was one of the first training officers in the Irish Civil Service. Essentially, my job was to teach effective communication, including writing, talking, negotiation, and explaining the workings of the different institutions of government. I needed to use whatever technical aids were available to me, such as blackboards, flip charts and overhead projectors. I also used to prepare 'how-to' handouts on a variety of subjects for distribution. That all added up to a structured form of working, with clearly defined objectives.

When my life was transformed and I began to develop my communication with guides, I had to adapt to a totally different style. In the early stages I was inclined to try to pin things down in the 'how-to' formula with which I was familiar; however, I soon found that this was like going down a blind alley. My usual organisational skills were useless; for example, I discovered that there was no point in trying to prepare for individual meetings or talks by making notes. I needed to use a different form of preparation that involved relaxing as much as I could, and then asking for help from my guides. Each individual meeting had to be totally spontaneous, and I had to be absolutely relaxed and open-minded for them to work.

When I spoke to the public, my talks lasted about ninety minutes. I might have some ideas in my head – or a story or stories that I could tell, if I found they were relevant – but I never used notes. At all stages I needed to be in tune with my guides and with the audience. I'd have made that impossible if I had a prepared agenda. Accordingly, my talks were always spontaneous within the realm of communication with guides and how the members of the audience could be helped to do that for themselves.

Systems and detailed planning and organisation are needed in day-to-day life on earth. However, trying to extend that approach to direct communication with guides will inevitably leave us open to frustration and disappointment. One of the most important and wonderful features of life is that we all have our own individual styles. It is through those 'styles' that our guides try to communicate with us. For instance, in my own case communication mainly happens through feelings or impressions, rather than pictures or words.

An undiscovered land

A participant at one of my courses shared this little story with the group:

'An explorer found a beautiful, undiscovered land. When she returned to her home, she told her friends about this country, describing the valleys, hills, rivers, trees, animals and plants. She told them: "You must go there for yourselves. My words cannot do justice to that land."

Her friends were excited to hear about the land, and were keen to investigate for themselves. They asked her to draw them a map to guide their journey and to show them exactly where the land was. She refused, saying: "No, you must set out and find the way for yourselves. There are many different routes and I only know one of them."

However, they insisted and, after a time, she relented and drew a map for them. Her friends were intrigued by the map

---

and spent days planning for the journey, discussing which route they would take, and what the land would look like. But they delayed, deciding that they had first better prepare thoroughly for the trip. Perhaps, too, they needed to know more about maps, how to read them, how to understand what picture the map showed. Years passed, the map was studied, then copied and passed on to others. Schools were set up in map-reading.

The explorer was sad and went away. No one visited the land.'

In my opinion, this little story highlights how we allow an over-organised approach to life to overwhelm and even obliterate our spirit of adventure. Our conditioned analytical processes get us nowhere in our efforts to achieve the intrepid open-mindedness needed in effective communication with guides.

I like the following quotation from George Bernard Shaw: 'Man who listens to reason is lost. Reason enslaves all whose minds are not strong enough to master her.'

Handing over

At a relatively early stage in my communication with guides I was offered a simple way of giving and receiving help. This was the gist of it:

Imagine yourself in a circle with your guides, who are channelling into the circle all the unconditional love of the universe. Suppose you're concerned about relatives or friends or people who are either living or have passed on, or material matters, or whatever. Imagine them all in the middle of the circle with all that love flowing around them. You feel yourself in alignment with that love. Imagine it also flowing all around your immediate environment, your country, all the continents, spreading peace and harmony around the world. Stay with the feeling as long as feels comfortable for you.

When I do that exercise, which can be done anywhere, at any time, I can feel loving energy flowing around the circle, and it usually rocks me gently backwards or forwards or round and round. In doing the exercise I release all need for worry, and I'm cooperating in sending unconditional help to whomever and wherever it's needed in the simplest and most effective way.

I'm told by Shebaka that if only one person in a thousand was to do that exercise or something similar on a regular (i.e., daily) basis, the effect would be so powerful that within a relatively short time span – say, about fifty years or less – there would be no wars, no crime, the freedom of the individual would be respected, and planet earth would be a wonderfully harmonious place. Why? Because of the flow of unconditional love around the universe and the consequential raising of global consciousness.

Since I was given that exercise, I have been doing it with the people I have met in individual sessions, in courses and in talks. To me, it's the best form of communication I can recommend. One of its most appealing aspects is that it involves no effort at all. I'm all for making things easy. An important feature of it for me is that I can feel the presence of my guides and let my analytical side take a rest.

One of the most common pleas that I heard from people during individual consultations and working with groups is that they needed to change their current situation and didn't know how. The first, and most important, answer is that there is nothing – no situation – that cannot be changed. The phrase 'thinking outside the box' has come into common usage and it is actually a remarkably apt way to describe what we need to do in our lives on a daily basis in order to open our minds and effect change. We need to let go of our linear ways of thinking and allow solutions to manifest – solutions at which we would never have arrived through our conditioned analytical processes.

My approach tended to be to ask people to suspend temporarily all thoughts of their present difficulties and then to make a list of what they enjoyed most. I suggested that they ask themselves how much those items featured in their day-to-day lives. In making their lists, I asked them to bear in mind that what they enjoy (or might enjoy, if they felt they had the opportunity to do so) doing today, they might not enjoy tomorrow.

The reason why I suggested making the lists is that by doing so they were focusing their energies, and looking at how they were living their lives. If, for example, they saw themselves as being trapped in a continuing round of duties, responsibilities, financial pressures, relationship problems, non-stimulating work, job worries and so on, they were locked into a negative pattern of energy that is self-perpetuating. My guides have always stressed that, no matter how much we may seem to be victims of circumstances, we still have the power to change our lives. That power is within us; we can exercise it positively or negatively. One thing is certain – there will not be positive direction in our lives unless we decide to make it so.

I next suggested that once they had made the decision to express themselves – focusing on how they could live in a manner that would provide them with creative fulfilment that would satisfy all the things they had outlined in their lists – they hand over the lists to their guides, symbolically, through their thoughts.

The handing-over process involves setting the wheels in motion to achieve support from the infinite, universal energy (unconditional love) in three ways. First of all, when we focus on what *we* want and need, and then take steps to hand this 'list' over to the guides, we are exercising our own free will. We are making decisions and choices. Secondly, we are providing positive direction to our energy, by outlining *how* we would like to express ourselves. We do this in the understanding that we are acting on our *present* perception of what we want, and allowing ourselves the flexibility to respond to our changing perceptions in the knowledge and trust that our guides are keeping a constant overview of our (soul) purpose. Finally, when we hand over, we are acknowledging that we need help. This is a liberating admission in itself, and literally opens us to receiving it.

It's important to remember that when we look back at our own physical journey on earth in our review of it, we are unlikely to be concerned by how many possessions we acquired, how much recognition we achieved or, indeed, our status. I am told that ultimately our only concern will be the extent to which we were able to release and enjoy our creative potential; in other words, our divinity.

When I ran my courses I could see very clearly how well the handing-over process worked. There are a few examples that stand out in particular.

Michelle was working in a business that she liked. She wrote on her list that she'd like to own the business. At the time, she knew that her financial situation was such that there seemed to be no hope of realising her dream unless the cost of the business would be no more than a certain amount that she wrote on her list. In a nutshell, she trusted in the handing-over process.

The course was spread over eleven weeks. One evening towards the end of it, she couldn't contain her excitement when she arrived. The owner of the business had approached her with an offer that he'd sell it to her for the exact amount that she had written on her list. She had handed over, and her dreams had been answered.

Another woman who achieved her dreams in the process of handing over was Carol, who longed for a baby. She put this on her list, and handed it over. On the last night of the course, at the end of the eleventh week, we had great cause for celebration. Carol was pregnant. Her husband was also on the course, and it may well be that his own aspirations combined with hers to make it an even more powerful process.

Another incident that springs to mind started with a long-distance call I had from a woman called Louise. She told me that she and her husband were due to pay a substantial debt by a certain date, and they had exhausted every means of finding the money. They had also looked for an extension of the deadline, but without success. It shouldn't have made any difference, but I felt more pressurised by the fact that she was ringing from another continent. I could only do my usual thing of handing the situation over to my guides. I asked her to do the same thing with her guides, and I assured her that a solution would emerge.

About three weeks later she telephoned me again to say that there had been no development, and there was now only a week to go before the money was due. There was still no hope of postponing the date of payment, so what were they going to do? Somewhat less confidently I told her that the message I was getting was that there was no need to worry.

Less than two weeks later I heard from her again. On the date that the debt was due to be paid, her husband received a completely unexpected refund of income tax, which was just enough to clear the debt. Once again, faith in the guides was justified.

Another woman told me about the way of working with her guides that she had developed. Whenever she felt that she needed help with a problem or a decision – or, indeed, anything – she wrote a note of thanks to her guides for the expected help and put it in a box. Then she followed her feelings, always with positive results.

This woman's story reminded me that I have so often forgotten to say thanks throughout my life. I don't mean just to guides, or to God/unconditional love, but for the wonder of life and all the beauty it offers daily in all sorts of ways. I thoughtlessly take so much for granted. Feeling and expressing gratitude create an expansive vibration that spreads all around us.

Occasionally in my talks I used the story of the fifth Labour of Hercules to reinforce my belief in the power of handing over apparently intractable problems to guides.

Hercules was tasked by King Augeas to clean out his stables, commonly known as the Augean stables, in a single day. I don't know how many stables there were, but I imagine that there were a lot of them – enough, anyway, to make it obvious that it would be impossible for him to clean out the accumulation of manure and filth in them in the allotted time, and with the tools available to him. Then he had an inspiration, which he followed. He went up to the top of a hill overlooking the stables and he found that there was a river running nearby. He went back down to the stables and knocked holes in the walls. Then he went up the hill again and managed to divert water from the river down the hill. The water gathered force as it flowed down the hill and in through the holes of the walls of the stables, sweeping clear all in front of it.

The story doesn't say what happened to the holes in the walls. Presumably he filled them up again! What it does tell us is that as notoriously strong as Hercules was, he could not do the job by himself. To me, the river in the story symbolises the universal flow of help that's available to us, which we can access ourselves or, ideally, through our guides, whenever we feel the need to do so.

Placing trust

These stories provide simple yet profound examples of how the spiritual and the material merge – how the material can be used as an aid to spiritual growth, and how, if we allow ourselves to trust enough, a lot of the hassle can be taken out of living and participating in the physical world. It's easy enough to trust, say,

50 or 80 per cent, but 100 per cent is a hard nut to crack. Yet, that's what is required. The universe doesn't know half measures. This may seem like an intimidating prospect, but we're assured that our guides always help us, no matter how doubting we may be. In our lack of trust, though, we deny ourselves the wonder of seeing things happen in often miraculous ways.

In our physical world, nothing exists in material form unless we *do* things. It's understandable then that we tend to see our image of ourselves by what we do – in other words going to the being from the doing. (That may be more true of men than of women.) In reality, what's important is *how* we are, in our being, when we do whatever it is that we do. The doing flows from the being. How we are is the important thing.

Working with guides has been a central feature in my life for many years, and I have found the handing-over process tremendously effective in making my life simpler and more rewarding. I don't want to pretend that I don't experience hassle, or get stressed about things, but that doesn't happen much. When it does, I remind myself to follow my usual practice.

I have been trying to explain as best I can the difference between the human and spirit ways of approaching things, and it is often difficult to get it across – particularly in the context of working with guides. Our conditioning as human beings leads us to expect that there are techniques that can be packaged and applied to every conceivable situation. In my experience I have never come across any methodology that will guarantee effective direct communication with guides in a way that can apply to everybody without exception. That's why I haven't tried to bring together into one chapter the whole area of communication with guides. Instead, I have let it run like a stream through the book, providing suggestions and examples from which people may find a way or ways that suit them.

For example, making lists is just one way of helping people to lead their lives in as fulfilling a way as possible. People may choose instead to ask in their heads. The important thing to remember is that whatever way people choose to communicate, they need to be as relaxed and their minds as still as possible.

Relaxation is a key factor in all communication with spirits – including loved ones – who have passed over. Various settings may be suitable for different people. For example, some may prefer an outdoor situation, while others may find indoors more suitable. Practice will soon show which setting is suitable for each person. Being in bed may be fine, but there could be a risk of falling asleep before anything happens!

The following is an extract from a communication that I received many years ago from Shebaka. I'm including it because I found it very helpful and informative in coming to terms with what was, at that stage, a comparatively new philosophy of living for me.

'It would be a great mistake to think that in asking for help and advice from your guides in coping with the daily challenges of life you would in some way diminish yourself or your capacity to make decisions for yourself. You cannot but increase your wisdom and decision-making capacity by reaching out towards a higher consciousness than your own. In a very real sense, the more you tune in to guidance the more self-reliant you become, because you begin to realise that you have immediate access to all the answers you need. Thus, the living of life becomes a simple and enjoyable process. You are making the best possible decisions in harmony with the universal scheme of things, and you know that you are doing exactly what you set out to do with your life.'

Shebaka went on to say that people who choose to relive an earth experience for the sake of repeating a pleasurable sensation do not usually wish to have guides helping them. They may not be at all interested in growth in awareness or spiritual development. However, if at any stage during their earth lives they change their minds, there are many enlightened souls willing and only waiting to be asked to act as guides. Shebaka says:

'For such is the universal love of which we are each a part, we are only being true to our own natures if we help each other. And in helping each other we also, of course, help

ourselves. None of us exists independently of another, which is often hard to accept in the daily commerce of living, particularly when a situation of antipathy arises between people.'

We can all improve our lives immeasurably by learning to ask – and to listen. Most of all, perhaps, it can be a great help to put our faith in the guides – our guardian angels, if you like – and to trust. Sometimes that's not easy, but it's well worth trying.

Chapter 5

Reincarnation

Reincarnation is a concept that has continued to intrigue humanity since the beginning of time. It remains a common belief among Eastern religions and philosophies, and was an integral part of Christian faith until it was removed by the Second Council of Constantinople in 553 AD. Since that time it has never been officially accepted by the Catholic Church – or, indeed, any of the major Protestant churches – although there can be no doubt that many Christians continue to believe that reincarnation exists.

There is something both exciting and frightening about the idea that the soul of a person whose body has died may be born again into another body at another time. In some ways it represents a second chance. For some people it explains feelings, instincts or characteristics that they have, which don't make sense in the context of their current lives.

Although not used on his tombstone, Benjamin Franklin's epitaph for himself is an interesting example of the belief in reincarnation. Benjamin Franklin was a printer, and one of the founding fathers of the USA. He wrote:

> The body of B. Franklin,
> Printer,
> Like the Cover of an Old Book,
> Its Contents Torn Out
> And
> Stripped of its Lettering and Gilding.
> Lies Here,
> Food For Worms
> But the Work shall not be Lost,
> For it Will as He Believed
> Appear Once More
> In a New and more Elegant Edition
> Revised and Corrected
> By the Author

Benjamin Franklin seemed sure that he would be back.

Returning in the future

Perhaps it's not surprising that when the subject of reincarnation comes up for discussion some people dismiss it on the basis that it boosts self-importance. Many people would probably feel rather grand if they believed they were kings or queens, or equally important people, in past lives.

Obviously, some people will have held important positions in past lives; however, those people may also have held servile positions in other lifetimes. My experience, through dealing with people and through what I've read about regressions (undergoing hypnosis in order to access information about past lives), there have been few instances of anything other than very ordinary existence. In truth, the only significance in finding out about previous lifetimes is their relevance to the present ones, for example, in helping people to be more tolerant in their dealings with others.

Margaret Anna and my other spirit guides state, without equivocation, that reincarnation exists. They present a picture of a soul evolving through a succession of physical lifetimes and, ideally, growing in awareness in each one. Of course, because our lives are dictated by our own free will, ideal growth may not be achieved in some lifetimes.

So what if reincarnation didn't exist? What if a soul is created for each new body and continues to exist after the death of the body, waiting around for Judgment Day when it will be reunited with its miraculously resurrected body? Is this a point when ultimate fate is decided – eternal happiness with God or eternal punishment with the devil? This is largely what many people have been taught to believe, and it presents a rather different picture to the idea of the soul evolving through a series of lifetimes.

There is, of course, a third option – that there is nothing beyond the death of the physical body. When we die we simply stop existing. Many people hold this belief, but for me it's a dispiriting one.

I have no doubt about the option of reincarnating as, ideally, a method of growth in awareness. I have been given many proofs of continuing life, some of which I have already outlined, and others that I'll describe later. In any case, as the woman in the bus said to me, I'll know soon enough.

If the prospect of being reincarnated is at all frightening, it's worth remembering that we have options and choices. The spirit guides have reassured me constantly that free will is always exercised when our spirits leave our bodies. In fact, free will is sacrosanct. No soul is forced to do anything it doesn't want to do, including reincarnating.

In fact, once any one of us accepts the fact that life continues, and in the way we wish it to, it seems nonsensical that we could be judged for eternity on the acts we undertake in one physical life. Our lifetime is merely the blink of an eye in 'eternal' terms. What's more, there are huge inequalities in the conditions in which we are born and we live. How could people be fairly and equally judged unless those considerations are taken into account? So rather than being fearful of the idea that we go on – and live again after our physical life on earth – we can rejoice in the idea that there is no Judgment Day looming, that the mistakes we made can be rectified to the best of our ability, and will not come back to haunt us.

Remembering the past

So why can't we remember our past lives, or even some of them? I have met people who remember whole swathes of earlier lives, and others who have odd memories that are clearly from a different lifetime. There are many recorded examples of cases where young children retain past-life memories. Over thirty years, Dr Ian Stevenson of the University of Virginia has done extensive research into children's spontaneous memories of past lives. His work provides details of about 100 stories of past-life reports from all over the world, which he followed up and found to be irrefutable. It seems that as children grow up the memories fade.

However, most people don't remember anything at all. Why is this? It's a question that I have put to my spirit guides on many occasions, and in particular the three guides with whom I speak regularly. They obviously don't work exclusively with me. Their reach is far more global than that. But when I need them they are there, and they reliably present answers to my questions. In this case, they've made it very clear that we forget in order to be given a fresh start – without the burdens that each lifetime offers. We are able to start again without guilt, fears, worries, habits, responsibilities or anything else. It is a great mercy that we are spared the memory of some of the happenings of the present life, not to mention being reminded of events from previous lives over which we'd prefer to draw a veil.

A very important point to bear in mind about reincarnation is that, if we accept it as a possibility, it ought to be helpful for us to free ourselves from all aspects of discrimination, whether racial, religious, gender-based or otherwise. It would be foolish to discriminate against one group or another when there's a chance that in a previous life or lives we could have been members of such groups.

Former life connections

Over the years, a number of different cases have come to my attention through individual consultations. All have served to open my mind to the possibilities that may transpire after we pass on.

Brenda came to see me after giving birth to a much-longed-for baby boy. She wondered if I could get information about any former life connections she and her husband might have had with their son.

The impressions I received from my guides were that Brenda's son, whose name was Sean, had been her son in a former life. He had been taken from her for reasons of social stigma and placed in a type of orphanage run by nuns. The chaplain to the community took a special interest in the boy and established a loving relationship with him. In the present life he was the boy's father. Brenda was delighted to hear that.

A few years later Brenda came to see me again. She told me that one day her son, then a little over 3 years old, turned to her suddenly and said, 'I knew Dad before. I was in a big house and he minded me. I didn't know you at all then, Mum – you weren't there.' He also said that Dad (as he was then) wore funny clothes.

I liked hearing Brenda's story, partly because it confirmed the impressions I had originally received, but also because it showed how love breaks down the barriers of time. What must have been a horrendous experience for Brenda in her former life had been transformed into one of joy in her present life. I was very grateful to her for having returned to tell me what Sean had said.

One morning I happened to turn on a radio station and an item about a man named Nigel (his real name – he gave me permission to use it), whom I knew, caught my attention. Some years earlier Nigel had come to see me. During our session I had informed him that I was getting an impression from my guides that he had been a prolific artist in late nineteenth-century France. I suggested that if he took up painting he'd be likely to find that his talent would manifest itself again in his present life. When something like this had previously come up, I usually found that the people in question did have a particular leaning or talent in the direction suggested. In other words, they had ability to write, act, paint, nurse or whatever.

In this case, Nigel had never even remotely considered painting. He found it hard to believe that he might have any artistic talent. Nonetheless, through seeming coincidences, he got an opportunity to join an art class, where he struck up an immediate rapport with the teacher. He was surprised at how quickly his efforts took shape. Within a relatively short period of time he sold several paintings, and he graciously invited me to open an exhibition of his work.

At present there's no way of proving that Nigel was a nineteenth-century French artist. What's incontrovertible is that he opened up a rich vein of untapped creativity through trusting that his guides were communicating valuable information to him.

Brenda's and Nigel's experiences are very different, and yet, they illustrate how a little faith in the concept of reincarnation can reap rewards. Learning about where their spirit had been in previous lives had allowed them to make deeper connections and appreciate their lives in a different way. Brenda had to bear the acute pain of separation from her son in her earlier life, but if she had known then that she would have the possibility to reunite with him – again as her son – in a later life, that knowledge would surely have given her some consolation. For most of us, the pain of bereavement is softened by the knowledge that it is not the end.

Similarly, one of the things that Nigel's case highlights is that it is all too easy to jog along in our lives in a state of resigned frustration (although this was not applicable to Nigel himself) – resigned because we can see no way of changing the direction of our lives, without causing huge upheavals of one kind or another. Yet perhaps it is easier than we think. Perhaps change is already within us, and waiting to be unfurled. Nigel's case was simple, but in many ways incredibly moving. Even though he was completely sceptical of his potential, he did open himself to the possibilities, and discovered untapped creativity that had lain dormant for centuries.

We are here for a purpose

Here on earth, grief is unavoidable, and its potential causes too plentiful to mention. Loss of money, freedom, health, relationships, status, friends, sporting contests, prestige and power can all cause us to grieve, and the intensity with which we do so varies between different people. Separation is probably one of the most common and distressing causes of grief, and, as the most final separation, death causes the most grief of all. How death occurs – through illness, violence, accidents or even suicide – most definitely impacts upon our burden of grief, and so too does the confusion we feel about the tragedies we experience. We can't help but wonder why there are such tragic happenings in the world, and why we are the recipients of such grief.

If we have an orthodox or traditional concept of God being a supreme being at the heavenly controls, we wonder how He could allow such awful things to happen in the world. If He is a loving Being, it simply doesn't follow that He could tolerate events that are capable of causing such pain.

But it isn't really as simple as that. Ultimately, it is our own free will – and how we use it – that affects the pattern of our lives. Margaret Anna has been very clear about this, and it is therefore possible to glean some understanding of why our lives unfold the way they do. I'll look at that a little later. For now, however, I think the whole question of reincarnation is worth considering in helping us to broaden our minds and make it easier to see why certain things happen – even what we regard as being tragedies. It's all part of the ways our souls evolve and learn.

I remember the case of a couple who were grief-stricken because of the loss of their young child. While I couldn't take away their grief, I got information from my guides that the child deliberately chose to be born to them so that their grief would leave them more open to exploring different avenues of how to exist in the world in a more meaningful way. Their reaction to that information could have been sceptical, or even hostile, but it wasn't. In fact they found it comforting, which is why I assumed the guides considered it important to pass it on to them.

Don't wait till the future

I don't mean to suggest that people should be resigned to continuing boring, restrictive or even desperately unhappy situations in the belief that they will have opportunities to find fulfilment in later lifetimes. My spirit guides, including Margaret Anna, have repeatedly made clear that we all *deserve* to be happy and that ultimately everybody will be.

Sometimes this is a difficult concept to accept, particularly in hugely difficult personal situations, and in global conditions where poverty, cruelty and all sorts of atrocities abound. But there are many people who work unobtrusively and often anonymously to create better conditions for those who are ill, poverty stricken, suffering from disabilities and generally under-privileged. That was what Margaret Anna set out to do in her last physical life and what she is still doing, along with millions of other souls. There's always help available once we're open to asking for, and receiving, it.

Why do some people have miserable lives? To answer that it would be necessary to have access to all the Akashic records of their evolution. Akashic is the title given to spirit (non-material) records of the evolutionary journeys of souls on their individual paths. Some light will be shone on this matter later in the book.

When Margaret Anna and I first discussed reincarnation, it was in the context of talking about proof of life after earth. She told me that many souls have returned – and continue to do so – as they are reincarnated. She also said that they don't usually remember their previous existences.

When she was describing her reunion with Charles Holmes, her fiancé, she said that neither of them would reincarnate again. She added: *'You might say that these communications are a sort of reincarnation!'*

I said, 'Many people don't believe in reincarnation. And, of course, it's not comprehended by the Christian tradition – at least since the sixth century. You obviously take it for granted.'

She replied, *'Yes. When I was last on earth it wasn't something that impinged on my consciousness. I was more concerned with existing conditions and how to fix them there and then. But it's a fact of life. I know – I've done it many times.'*

I didn't ask her for any details of her past lives. I assumed that she'd have given them to me if she thought they were relevant to what we were doing. Anyway, I'd only have been asking out of idle curiosity.

I suggested to her that she may, over time, change her mind and return again, but she was adamant that her choice was absolute. She said, *'I feel I can play a more significant part in helping to raise consciousness by staying put. I don't mean that to be taken generally – I'm just speaking for myself.'*

She explained that we all make our own decisions as our souls evolve. Sometimes we don't progress in a particular incarnation and may choose to reincarnate. The key is to free ourselves from what we've been taught about God as a separate, remote being, and to develop as souls, over several lifetimes, until eventually we move into a place of complete and perfect harmony. In Margaret Anna's case, she has nothing more to learn from earthly life and has progressed spiritually to a stage where she's working as a spirit guide in a totally unconditionally loving way.

Chapter 6

Spirit Guides at Work

Once a complete mystery, the workings of the spirit guides have begun to become clear to me over the years. My communication with Margaret Anna in particular has been resoundingly enlightening, as well as enormously reassuring, and it is through her words that I can best describe how the spirit guides effect the changes in our lives that they do, and how they communicate both with us and among themselves.

I was communicating with Margaret Anna one evening when I realised that I had interrupted the flow several times. I stopped to apologise, and she asked me not to do so any more.

'I'm not controlled by time like you,' she said. And so it was that I began to view our communications in a different way. They were also shaped by Margaret Anna's view of memory. She doesn't have memory lapses, she said, so she has no *need* for memory.

She said, *'There's nothing I need to forget so I can forgo the protective screen of memory.'*

This is an interesting concept. In the human state we think of memory as the capacity to remember things, whereas it's interesting to see it as an aid to *forgetting* things that we have no need to remember. In particular, it can be an aid to forget things that are often a source of guilt and depression. Speaking for myself at least, I think that one of the benefits of growing old is that a selective process takes place about what I need to remember instead of putting energy into dwelling on things that are usually of very temporary significance.

What's in a name?

Margaret Anna commented to me about how many recorded spirit communications are from souls with exotic-sounding names, such as the names of Native American chieftains and so forth. She felt that people might relate more easily to communications from someone with a non-exotic name like hers: Margaret Anna Cusack. She said, *'It's ordinary, like everyman or everywoman.'*

I'm not so sure about that myself. The concept of spirit guides (or guardian angels) can seem far-fetched for some people, and I think we are all guilty of being slow to accept that extraordinary information can come from apparently ordinary sources. Maybe it's because we don't think enough of ourselves to accept that people with ordinary names can be capable of extraordinary things. Exotic names somehow make it more convincing!

No spiritual hierarchy

When people get together to work on any project – political, social, religious or whatever – the first thing they do, almost inevitably, is to set up an organisation with rules and regulations and pyramids of hierarchical positions. In many religions we are told of a hierarchy of angels. In Christianity, for example, angels fall into orders, or 'angelic choirs'. Is this actually the way that angels operate?

Margaret Anna has been very clear about this point, and she has stressed that nobody – including other souls in spirits – tells her what to do. She feels that it is important to establish this, because it is an all-too-common belief that there is a type of ruling hierarchy in spirit, who assign missions to their minions. So the structures that dictate our life on earth no longer exist. How do they operate?

According to Margaret Anna, guides have what she calls a 'cooperative system'. It would be unthinkable for them to sit idly by while people struggle. There are hordes and hordes of souls in spirit engaged in all sorts of schemes designed to help their brothers and sisters on earth. They have conferences and they set up committees. They choose the ways in which they'd like to help, bearing in mind the areas that most suit them. They may decide to appoint a coordinator who will keep an overview of their different programmes and, of course, they meet frequently to discuss how they're progressing.

Margaret Anna says, *'While we're very aware of human traumas and the suffering that many of our human "charges" are experiencing, and we certainly don't take them lightly, nevertheless, because we can see the bigger picture, we retain our feelings of joy and are in what I might describe as states of concerned detachment. We wouldn't be much help to anybody if we got caught up emotionally in every passing crisis.'*

Here, for a reason that will become obvious later, I'd like to mention a friend of mine, Frank. I had come to know him when a mutual friend introduced him to me, after which we had established a great rapport. He was a member of the Catholic religious Order of Marist Brothers. He had qualified as a teacher and worked in Africa for many years, doing rehabilitative work as well as teaching. In his youth he had been an active and talented footballer. When he read them he was very taken with my books and used them in his work of helping recovering male addicts. He had died a few years ago, but on a number of occasions he has communicated freely not just with me but also with another mutual friend. He has been invariably accurate in all his communications. He is now participating in the type of cooperative system referred to by Margaret Anna, by easing the passing of souls into their new situation.

What crisis?

It's comforting to know that when we are in our darkest hour there is someone looking out for us. But in spirit they look at things rather differently. Margaret Anna has said that what humans see as crises aren't really crises at all. She had her own share of crises when she was on earth, and concedes that this may not be a particularly helpful statement for anyone going through what they perceive to be traumatic times. However, it's fair to say that when we look back we often wonder why we got so worked up over situations that, in hindsight, seem trivial. From the guides' perspective on the mountaintop, as it were, they can see the purpose behind the happenings, they rejoice in the understanding that sometimes comes later on, and are so grateful when they can help people to reach that understanding.

Margaret Anna says, *'We have great fun here. Don't let anybody think for a minute that we're clones of each other. We're able to express our different and unique personalities in ways that we didn't feel free to on earth. And I think you can gather from the tone of my communications, even though you're putting them into rather careful language, that I'm anything but a pietistic, antiseptic type of individual.*

'However, it would be misleading of me to present a picture of life in spirit as full of uninterrupted joy. It is for many, according to their states of awareness. But, unfortunately, there are still many souls in spirit who are experiencing what I can only call the tortures of hell, except that, mercifully, we know that it's only a temporary hell. The duration of it

is determined by how willing they are to open themselves to a new awareness of themselves.'

I wondered what she could mean. What could lead to souls in spirit experiencing the tortures of hell? She agreed to give me some examples.

Unhappy souls

In the religious teaching of my youth, suicide was regarded as a mortal sin that meant punishment by hellfire for all eternity. Any person who committed suicide wasn't entitled to be buried in consecrated ground. I shudder to think that so many people – and, I'm ashamed to say, I was once one of them – subscribed to such a belief system. For all I know, many may still do.

Margaret Anna described the case of a man whom she called Johann, who was born into a well-to-do family in Austria in the early part of the twentieth century. He qualified as a doctor and went to work and live in Germany. His move to Germany coincided with the rise to power of the Nazis. He was an ideal-istic young man who saw his medical career as a vocation rather than a job. He couldn't but be aware of the changing political scenario, but he was so absorbed in his work that, to some extent, it passed him by; until, that is, he was drawn into it.

He was given a commission in the German army, which initially was quite pleasing to him. He saw this as an opportunity to give whatever healing he could to wounded soldiers. However, he wasn't allowed to stay in that role for long. His new assignment was to examine imprisoned Jews in order to select those who, in his opinion, were fit for manual work.

His instructions were clear – selection or rejection. In the early stages he was unaware of what happened as a result of his decisions. Inevitably, of course, he found out, and his horror was indescribable. Johann went to his superior officer and requested that he be transferred to another post where he could fulfil his medical vocation. He got an unambiguously direct answer: 'Go back to your post or you'll be shot as a traitor.' After much agonising he went back and tried to convince himself that he was doing his patriotic duty – that maybe the authorities had access to information he didn't, which indicated that Jews were in some sinister ways seeking to undermine the stability of the State. He became as efficient a robot as he could.

The years went by, the war eventually ended, and the extent of the Nazi atrocities began to be revealed to the world. Johann could no longer anaesthetise himself. He sought oblivion and committed suicide in 1947. But, of course, there was no oblivion. He couldn't get away from himself. The realisation that he couldn't destroy himself, that he had no choice but to live with himself indefinitely, was the source of the most agonising mental torture for him – a despair that knew no relief.

Margaret Anna took on the task of helping Johann to a point where he could begin to accept, if not to love, himself. The first and most important part of her task was to help him to unburden himself. Johann was racked with guilt, and in his own eyes he was utterly worthless. He felt that he had completely reneged on his vocation and betrayed his profession through his cowardice; he had saved his own life at the cost of many, many others.

In the early stages of their contact, Johann wouldn't even acknowledge Margaret Anna. But she continued to turn up – sitting silently near him, projecting love at him, just being with him. After some time he began to look at her somewhat furtively. Eventually he asked her what she wanted.

'*Nothing,*' she said. And that was the end of their conversation. They continued to sit silently together.

Margaret Anna didn't stay with him continuously; she kept coming and going, so that he had long periods by himself. She noticed that, in spite of his resistance, he couldn't disguise his pleasure when she turned up. He was slowly beginning to enjoy contact with someone else, who was obviously not looking at him with abhorrence, which was how he was feeling about himself.

When she felt that the time was right, she told him that she was with him as a representative of divine love and that she wanted to help him to forgive himself and enjoy being alive and well.

'*How can I forgive myself?*' he asked in torment. '*You don't know all the terrible crimes I have committed, all the suffering I have caused.*'

'Yes, I do. I know everything,' she replied.

After a long pause he asked, *'And yet you don't reject me?'*

Margaret Anna assured him that he was now in a dimension where he would meet no rejection. Haltingly, he began to talk, to let all his self-recrimination pour out, and she listened. She let him talk away. She could see him observing her, wondering if she was horrified by what he was telling her. As he saw that there was no change in the way that she was relating to him, he became more expansive and there were even occasional glints of humour.

Gradually things evolved to the stage where he agreed to let her take him to meet other souls, who accepted him unquestioningly. He began to allow himself to enjoy their company spontaneously. She no longer has to come and get him. He automatically connects with the group, or with one or more of them, as he wishes.

I wondered about the victims of his selections; would he have to face them? She said that sooner or later it would happen – as it does on earth. What did that mean, I wondered?

Margaret Anna answered, *'People don't realise – mercifully – that they're in frequent, often daily, contact with some who have abused them in some form or another in a previous life or previous lives. The reverse is also true – they may be in contact with people they have abused. It's never all one-way traffic. Johann may eventually choose to reincarnate into an environment where he will have opportunities to make restitution in some form to one or more of his victims and, through*

84

them, to humanity as a whole. That will be his choice. Opportunities other than reincarnation will also be available to him. The main thing is that he's on his way.'

Souls communicating

I have to confess to interrupting Margaret Anna's story about Johann. She spoke at length about the conversations they had, and I was curious to know what she meant by 'talking' in spirit. She informed me that languages, as we know them, are unnecessary in spirit.

She said, *'We function through thought transmission.'*

Margaret Anna reminded me that in our communication she wasn't using any words; instead, she was transmitting thoughts to me and I was interpreting them into *my* words. I now understand that souls can operate at whatever level they wish – using books, words or any other form of communication without limitation. In a way, the idea of books shows how our own communication on earth is limited, and how spirit can transcend that. Margaret Anna says:

'There will always be writers and books and readers. Suppose you go into a bookshop where there are books in many different languages. If you open a book that is, say, written in Swedish, it will be incomprehensible to you because you have

> *no knowledge of Swedish. Imagine, though, that you have reached a stage at which when you open the Swedish book you automatically understand the Swedish words, although you have never studied the language. It's hard to grasp from where you're sitting. We can operate at whatever level we wish. Those who like to use words will continue to do so. It's not an either/or situation. Limitation of possibilities only applies to your present human thinking. There's no need to try looking around corners that don't exist. There's nothing to stop you having the best of all worlds.'*

Visits from unhappy souls

In my individual sessions with people, souls who had committed suicide occasionally came through. Sometimes they were confused because, of course, they had sought oblivion and hadn't found it. They were just wandering around frequenting old haunts, like public houses or bookmakers' offices, and trying to talk to people who couldn't see or hear them, which left them feeling very lonely and frustrated. I would suggest to them that they look for a light that would lead them to a guardian angel who would look after them. I'm glad to say that this usually worked.

Others weren't confused at all. They had responded to the help that was always available to them from their guides and/or groups, such as Frank's. Their purpose in coming through was to reassure their loved ones in the physical world that they were fine, and to express their regret for the pain that they had caused them by leaving so abruptly. Those who were left behind, particularly parents, often blamed themselves – and believed that they were somehow responsible for not noticing that there was any problem. Even though it was still difficult for them to get over the pain of separation and, particularly, the awful abruptness of it, they now had the consolation that their son or daughter or friend was alive and well.

I remember one unusual case. A young man who believed without reservation in continuing life was impatient to find out what it was like. He jumped off a wall with fatal consequences for his body. He came through to reassure his mother that he was in good form, except that he regretted that he couldn't get back the same way that he had left. He would have to go through the whole process of reincarnation again (if, of course, he wished to do so). This was one soul who had not learned the art of patience.

Rightly or wrongly, I have come to the conclusion that the increasing incidence of suicide has been compounded by the fact that many souls find the density and restrictiveness of living in physical bodies on earth too much for them, after having experienced the freedom of spirit. Of course, this brings up the question of why any soul bothers to be born into such challenging situations. But, clearly, it's all to do with raising levels of consciousness or awareness. An effective way to do this is to be forced up against a wall, so to speak, so that we have no choice but to try to liberate ourselves and find freedom in the way we think. Trying circumstances often bring out the best in people, and always teach a lesson.

Forebodings of death

Many of us fear death, even when we are reassured that there is something profoundly wonderful that follows. There are multiple stories of people who have had premonitions or forebodings of imminent death – and not usually their own death, either. In Ireland there used to be (maybe there still is) a tradition surrounding what is known as a 'banshee'. My dictionary describes this creature as a 'female spirit whose wailing warns of a death in a house'. Literally, the word 'banshee' means a 'woman of the fairies'. As far as I know, it's a mythical tradition that applies only to certain families.

There was a road leading to the house where I was brought up. At one of its turns, the banshee was believed to sit combing her hair. I remember hearing a story about a foolish man who snatched her comb and ran as fast as he could into his house. Hot on his heels, the banshee pursued him, and arrived wailing at the door. Realising the mistake he had made, he was about to hand her the comb, but the woman of the house stopped him. She placed the comb on some tongs and handed it to the banshee. As the banshee took the comb, the tongs broke in half. I expect the man was very grateful he hadn't handed them over directly, and that he suffered no ill effects after the risk he took.

I tried to avoid travelling on that road as much as I could but sometimes I had no choice. I usually approached the 'famous' corner in a state of utter trepidation and, without looking to the right or left, I ran as fast as I possibly could until I felt I was safe. Although I felt sorry for the poor banshee having to sit there on her own, day and night, I was absolutely terrified of seeing her. Certainly if I had there was no chance that I'd attempt to snatch her comb.

History and mythology are full of warnings or forebodings of death. I never heard of anybody who actually saw a banshee and chances are that people won't come across a banshee forecasting the death of a loved one, but there are many stories of deaths being foretold in other ways.

One woman, Elizabeth, told me how she had a vivid dream of chasing over some sort of wire netting – following somebody who was going so fast that she didn't know who it was. She managed to get over some of the wires, but eventually she came to one that foiled her. She woke up with a start and saw her mother smiling down at her from the ceiling of the bedroom. Simultaneously, there was a loud knocking at her front door. When she opened the door, a neighbour told her that the hospital had phoned to tell her to come immediately – that her mother was seriously ill.

Needless to say, when she arrived at the hospital her mother had already passed away. She had, however, found her own way of telling her beloved daughter about her death – and showing her that she had made the transition. She had made it clear to Elizabeth that she would continue to be a smiling, loving presence in her life.

I was personally involved in another story that didn't include a premonition, as such, but, rather, advance information. I can't remember whether it was on a Sunday or a Monday that I got a message for a woman named Laura. The message was from her father, who had died years previously. He told me that Laura's mother would leave her body on the following Thursday. It was not usual for me to get this type of information, and I would normally have been hesitant about passing it on, but in this case Laura's father impressed on me that it was very important that I give her the message. So I did. Laura's mother was ill with cancer and was in hospital, but she didn't seem to be in any imminent danger of dying. Laura had an appointment that kept her late on the Wednesday but, even though she was very tired, she felt impelled to visit her mother. She was the last visitor her mother had before she passed away early on Thursday morning. In this case the warning eased some of the grief that Laura experienced at her mother's death.

It is interesting that animals seem to get all sorts of premonitions of forthcoming events – in particular, floods or tsunamis, and other natural disasters – and also seem to be able to sense the impending death of humans and other animals. Because of our analytical conditioning, we usually tend to ignore such feelings, which is a great pity. We've lost sight of our hunches and gut feelings; when we pick up impressions, we argue ourselves out of them or allow them to be buried under the weight of all the other earthly concerns we carry around.

My father was the youngest of fourteen children. He never knew some of his siblings, as they had emigrated to America before he was born. In those times something called 'the American wake' was a common event. People had to emigrate for economic reasons mainly, but I'm sure there was also a hope of finding gold at the end of a rainbow – not just in a financial sense but also in a romantic one. America was the land of opportunity where people of even the humblest of origins could aspire to the top of the tree, as it were. Wakes were held (and still are, in some places, as far as I know) when someone has died. It may seem odd that a wake would be held when someone was simply leaving Ireland for another country, but in the nineteenth century America was very much 'another world'. When someone left to emigrate to America it was very unlikely that they would ever return, no matter how good their intention to do so. Many of the emigrants completely lost touch with their Irish relatives.

If modern systems of communication had been in place, one can imagine how much easier it would have been for Irish families to say goodbye to their loved ones. Now imagine, too, what it would be like if advances in technology would make it as easy for us to communicate between the different dimensions – physical and non-physical – in much the same way that Ireland can communicate with America. Is it a bigger leap of the imagination than it would have been for a nineteenth-century Irish immigrant to America to conceptualise today's methods of communication? It would have seemed a world away, and probably impossible. Perhaps we should open our minds to the idea that we too may be able to communicate with the spirit world that easily.

Communication with the 'other world' would undoubtedly give us insight into how and why our lives unfold, and provide us with access to the almost limitless help that the spirit guides are able to offer. (In my experience, it does those things, but of course people have to find that out for themselves.) The more we learn about the other side, the more we are able to understand why things happen the way they do here on earth, and the more comforted we are by the prospect of a profoundly loving and happy existence after death. If we open our mind to the possibilities, anything can happen – and will.

Chapter 7

Opening Our Minds

Margaret Anna uses stories to illustrate various aspects of life in spirit. Through these stories I have acquired a wealth of detail about what life is like after death, as well as many of the tools necessary to make the transition from the physical to the non-physical world as seamless and as positive as possible. One thing to which Margaret Anna consistently drew attention in her stories is the fact that our state of mind is crucial not just to how we travel through life in our physical existence, but to how we move into the next. Being open-minded seems to be vital to the success of both.

Would having a closed mind affect our transition? And what if we were depressed when we died? Would we carry these things over to our non-physical life? Margaret Anna confirmed that there are many souls who continue to exist in states of depression and withdrawal. Our actions on earth impact on our lives beyond.

She commented on the case of Johann, the doctor mentioned in the previous chapter, who could be said to have been an 'abuser' through force of circumstances. While the effects of his decisions were devastating for many people, he acted under duress, and without any trace of malice. His true loving nature was masked by his unwillingness to put his own ideals above his personal safety. It's a common enough example of human frailty, but it was made much more dramatic by the scale of the operations in which he was involved.

Margaret Anna continued, *'Many people perform acts of horrific abuse and show no trace of remorse. Their way of life is totally based on their need for self-gratification, irrespective of how that can be achieved. Any concept of soul or spirituality is alien to them. They get vicarious enjoyment from exercising power over others and seeing them suffer.'*

When they reach spirit they can't bear to find that they are not still where they used to be and that they no longer have that power. Margaret Anna said that she had been dealing with someone like that and agreed to tell me his story.

The gang-leader who lost his gang

On earth, Alfredo was a vicious criminal, the head of a notorious gang who terrorised people. He was an active participant in every conceivable form of human degradation, and showed no mercy or regard for human life. Increasing age didn't mellow him; in fact, the reverse was true. Up until the day he died he was issuing ruthless orders with devastating effects on helpless people.

When he shed his body, Alfredo was lost. He no longer had the trappings of power that he had relished. There was no point in shouting for his lackeys – which he did endlessly. He was beside them, behind them, in front of them, but they couldn't hear him. One can imagine his frustration, and the threats of dire punishment that he poured out at them. But his minions ignored him. Alfredo was discovering that he was helpless, and to say he didn't like it would be a pretty large understatement.

It may be said, understandably, that Alfredo deserved to be left in that state indefinitely. Perhaps it could be considered an apt fate for a man who had caused so much suffering on earth. But things don't work like that in spirit, where there's no judgment. In reality, souls punish *themselves*, through their states of mind. That was what Alfredo was now doing.

Margaret Anna was there to support him but she was aware that only he could help himself. There was nothing she could do in the immediate sense except be patient. She did, however, stress that it was important to note that she didn't feel in any way superior to Alfredo. She said: *'I was in a different dimension of awareness and therefore in a position to help him whenever he would be ready to receive help. I understood that how Alfredo expressed himself in his earth life did not reflect his soul essence; his exercise of his free will had temporarily obscured it completely. My job was to help him to see that.'*

Margaret Anna said that he was so obsessed with what was going on with his gang that it was impossible for her to achieve any communication with him. This continued for a long time in our terms; several years, in fact. She tried various means of reaching him, including bringing along some of his relatives to see him. There were his parents, a grandmother he had loved as a child, and many others. Nothing worked.

But they who act as guides never give up. They can exercise endless patience because they have no concept of time, or any need to worry about it. They also have no agenda other than to help and guide, and show unconditional love for those around them and beyond. Spirit guides know, too, that there will inevitably be a breakthrough; with all the unconditional love they show, there simply has to be. Not surprisingly, there was eventually a breakthrough for Alfredo.

When Alfredo was a child, he had a playmate – a little girl. Margaret Anna called her Lucilla, and she was roughly the same age as Alfredo. They lived near one another and played together regularly. It came as a huge shock when Lucilla died at the age of 7, and Alfredo was deeply traumatised. Alfredo's grandmother also died, and Alfredo had no one left to whom he felt close.

By the time Alfredo had passed into spirit, Lucilla was, of course, no longer a little girl. As a soul, she had reverted to the way she used to be before her earthly life as Lucilla. However, the guides arranged that she would appear to Alfredo as he had known her. They had to choose their opportunity carefully because his obsession with what was going on with his former 'empire' had created around him what Margaret Anna might call an impenetrable brick wall. Sooner or later, Alfredo was going to have to let down his defences, if only for an instant, and the guides were watching him and ready. Eventually, such a moment arrived, and the guides snatched it. Alfredo became aware of Lucilla as the little girl she had been so many years earlier.

I couldn't help but wonder how the guides were able to change Lucilla's appearance, but Margaret Anna was quick to explain that it was simple. As she said, *'In spirit we can take on any appearance we like. All we need do is imagine it. People try to do that on earth, too, through plastic surgery, and different hairstyles, and even putting on new faces every day with make-up – but you wouldn't know anything about that, of course!'*

In case anybody might be tempted to ask how a nineteenth-century nun would know about such things as plastic surgery, I had better explain that Margaret Anna has, of course, long since moved on from that physical existence. It wouldn't be possible for her to act as a guide to humans if she wasn't well aware of conditions in the modern physical world. She hears and sees our problems and our lifestyles, and implicitly understands them, whatever their time in history.

I was slightly taken aback to hear about this 'shape-changing', and explained to Margaret Anna that I found it a bit disturbing. It would be strange, I thought, to communicate with a soul that was taking on different forms as we spoke. I felt that I would be on tenterhooks wondering to whom I was relating.

But Margaret Anna reassured me: '*No, you wouldn't really. The form is always consistent with our persona or our style so that we have no difficulty in recognising each other. You might understand more easily if you see it like an actor playing different roles on the stage, with appropriate make-up and costumes. The actor is still the same person. The central point here is that Alfredo wouldn't have known Lucilla in any other form.*'

Margaret Anna continued with her story of Alfredo, and explained that the transformation in him was remarkable. When he saw Lucilla, he briefly became a child again. They held hands and they danced and they laughed. As this happened, all of the intervening turbulence fell away from him – until he remembered and went behind his wall again. But a start had been made and gradually the wall came down. Lucilla's love had triumphed. There's still a long way for Alfredo to go. In our time it may take many centuries. However, once the barrier is down the rest will follow.

Margaret Anna has no direct involvement with Alfredo now. She acts as an orchestrator behind the scenes – something that guides often do. The outcome is what's important – not who achieves it.

Alfredo's story shows us that no soul can ever be lost, and the reason is that all souls are part of God – or, in other words, unconditional love. On earth, someone such as Alfredo would (or, some people would say, should) be sentenced to life imprisonment, a span of something like twenty years. However, Alfredo's mindset, which made him unprepared to move on in the spiritual dimension, meant that he actually punished himself for what might, in our terms, be centuries. His punishment was, in reality, far worse than anything that could be inflicted on earth. Before souls can ever be truly themselves – that is, no longer separate from their divine essence – they have to *face* themselves. They are given support and guidance in this process, and with that help they can release themselves from the prison of closed-mindedness and, perhaps, find a way to make reparation to the victims of their crimes.

When they can't get through

When guides find it difficult to get through to a person directly, they will attempt indirect approaches, often through other people. Margaret Anna says, *'We find another way; for example, by seeking the help of somebody close to our "charge" – somebody who would be more receptive to our prompting.'*

I asked whether having a 'direct line' was all that important then. Margaret Anna replied, *'In the long run, no. It can even be a hindrance if people set up an anxiety in themselves because they don't seem to be getting any obvious answers. Trust first, then leave the "hows" open. I'm presupposing, of course, that there's an acceptance that guides never fail those whom they've agreed to guide.'*

For me, that was a very important and relevant answer. Most
– if not all – of the people that I met wanted to have direct
communication with their guides. In many cases they
complained that no matter how hard they tried they simply
couldn't hear, see or feel anything. I could sympathise with
those feelings, of course. It can sometimes feel as if we are sending out messages into the ether with no real idea of what or
who is on the receiving end.

The real source of the problem is the act of 'trying'. Trying
creates anxiety if there's not an immediate or obvious answer.
Once this happens, a barrier is created against any possibility of
direct communication. Furthermore, when we look for direct
communication – which is what we are inclined to do when
we have a problem to which we want a particular solution – it
is difficult to be objective. We may actually be exerting control
on an unconscious level, so that we get the answer we want. All
this does, really, is set up frustration later on.

There's a story that emanates from somewhere in the East
that illustrates very vividly the difficulties that people create for
themselves in looking for direct communication.

On a little island there was a temple with a thousand bells.
The bells would tinkle in the wind, and there was a long-stand-
ing tradition that anybody who could hear them would know
God.

Years passed. At some stage there was a huge flood and the
temple was submerged in the sea surrounding the island. The

tradition remained, though: anybody who could hear the tinkle of the bells would know God. Sadly, for many years nobody heard the bells.

Eventually a young man decided that he was going to sit by the sea and listen until he could hear them. He found a tree under which he sat and sheltered. With great fervour he listened, but all he could hear was the wind whistling through the trees and the crashing of the waves endlessly coming into the shore and then receding. The sounds of nature constantly intruded on his silence.

The people in his neighbourhood, who knew of his vigil, brought him food and drink. Day passed day, night passed night, and weeks moved on into months. But, no matter how hard he concentrated, he couldn't hear even a little tinkle. After about six months he announced to the neighbouring inhabitants that he was giving up his quest.

Having made his decision, he relaxed and decided that he would pay a farewell visit to the tree, as a gesture of thanks for the shelter it had given him during his vigil. As he sat there he found that all of the familiar sounds of nature – the sea, the wind and the crashing waves – no longer jarred on him. He felt a great sense of peace and unity with them.

After a little while he heard what seemed like a little tinkle of a bell, and then another, and another, until there was a whole crescendo of bells tinkling. And then, so the story goes, he knew God.

The perception of happiness

At an early age in my communication with guides I was informed that three things were important – relaxation, patience and trust. In my experience, one or more of them, and often all three, created difficulties for people. So I would usually suggest not to bother looking for direct answers but to hand over to their guides whatever their problem was and to trust that a solution would emerge. I find that approach invariably works well for me. I usually only tend to look for direct answers when I'm writing – with Margaret Anna, for example. In such circumstances I know that there's no point in my sitting down to have any type of communication unless I'm completely relaxed.

Our mindset is important not just for communication, but also for the way in which we make the transition to spirit. We carry our mindsets with us when we pass on, and it is these that will define our experience in the next world – and how long it will take us to achieve perfect harmony with unconditional love.

Margaret Anna told me a story about a woman whom she called Monica. When she was on earth, Monica grew up in a deeply religious environment. From an early age there was never the slightest hint of a doubt in her mind that she would be a nun. In due course she entered a convent and subjected herself with total dedication to all of the disciplines of religious

life. She was an exemplary nun. She welcomed every assignment, no matter how tedious, and she willingly volunteered for
extra duties. She punished herself rigorously if she thought
she'd transgressed even the most minor regulations.

Monica was an obvious candidate for higher office, and in
the fullness of time she became the Superior of her Order. In
the discharge of her office she was as severe with others as she
was with herself. The rules were sacrosanct; the service of God
allowed for no laxity. Demonstrations of affection were taboo
because Monica's God had no time for smiles or hugs. She was
respected and feared, and she showed no vulnerability. Nobody
got close to her, but she was an excellent administrator and
believed that this was how she showed her love.

When the time came for Monica to hand over the reins of
office to somebody else, she did so willingly, in accordance with
the will of God, as she believed totally. She lived into her 80s
and died with all the comforts of religion, secure in the belief
that she was going to her due reward in Heaven for her faith-
ful service on earth.

Monica observed the funeral ceremonies and listened to the
tributes paid to her. There were no tears; there was no sadness
because of her departure. The whole affair was full of solem-
nity. It was all just as it should be, in Monica's view.

Margaret Anna had chosen to help Monica through her transition. She said that any approach that held even a hint of levity
would be inappropriate. *'It would never have done if I had appeared*

as a nun dressed in a miniskirt and wearing a stud in my nose, or something like that.' Margaret Anna decided that she would lay on all the style for Monica. Monica had lived her life in a spirit of total self-denial and service. She had fulfilled her side of a bargain with God, as she saw it, and there could be only one reward – Heaven. So Heaven was what she found when she passed on – that is, Margaret Anna's presentation of Heaven, as she believed Monica perceived it to be. She laid on a solemn religious ceremony with a phalanx of officiating dignitaries dressed in splendid ecclesiastical robes. A centrepiece of the ceremony was a special welcome for Monica. She was very pleased.

Next, Margaret Anna arranged that Monica would be introduced to members of her Order, who are now in spirit, and who tended to see life in much the same way as she did.

I asked Margaret Anna why she chose to lay on a type of theatrical production for Monica that might be said to be leading her up the garden path.

Margaret Anna replied, *'She was already dealing with the transition from physical to spirit life and leaving behind all the securities she had known within the confines of her Order. I felt that she needed to have the comfort of the fulfilment of her expectations until she was ready to open her mind to other possibilities. That was the sort of welcome she expected, and that's what she got. The mind creates its own reality. I was simply acting as an agent of her mind until she could let go of its rigidity. She was happy within her perception of happiness.'*

Perhaps, I wondered, Monica might be happiest staying like that indefinitely? Margaret Anna reminded me of what she'd said earlier: Monica was happy within *her perception of happiness.*

She said, '*The main snag was that she had suppressed the joy in her, the essence of her divine nature. My job, as I saw it, was to help her to open herself to that joy – that love. I did so gradually by appearing to her in my angelic paraphernalia – which I can tell you are very impressive! I took her to all sorts of gatherings – discussion groups, where often weighty topics were explored with much humour and laughter, dances, theatrical performances, concerts, all sorts of happenings. A feature of these was joyful expressiveness. She was a bit resistant at first, but she couldn't get past the status my angelic appearance gave me and she gradually relaxed and began to enjoy herself. Slowly, she let go of her rigidity and accepted that it was permissible for her to indulge herself in what would have previously seemed to her as perilously close to devilish temptations.*'

Monica's story reminded me of the seriousness with which religion was practised in my youth – and still is in lots of ways. For example, nobody played music or indulged in any kind of revelry for a month after a family member died. It might even have been a year; I can't remember now. Certainly people continued to wear severe mourning clothes, always black, for what seemed like ages afterwards. Why is it still a widespread custom for people to wear black clothes at funerals? Shouldn't we be celebrating a life on earth and the joys that will greet our loved ones when they pass on to spirit?

Joyful expression

One of the main objects of this book, which is entirely inspired by Margaret Anna, is to eliminate the fear of death and – even more important, I think – what happens after it. The level to which we can open our minds is the key to this.

Margaret Anna has set out to show what life is like in spirit. She has been able to define this 'other world' with some representative examples – including two totally dissimilar cases, Monica and Alfredo. At one end of the spectrum was Alfredo, who descended to the lowest levels of thuggery. At the other was Monica, who lived her life in total dedication to the implementation of God's will, as she understood it. In common parlance, Alfredo would be regarded as evil and Monica as good. Yet, apart from the fact that they were both human beings, they had one thing in common – closed-mindedness – which in both cases led to a lack of joyful expression in their lives.

Indulgences

In the early stages of my communication with guides, I was intrigued by the constant feeling of humour and joy that emanated from them. It seemed to be totally at odds with the concept of spirituality, as I had been conditioned to know it. Certainly, in my experience, religion did not seem to have much joy in it. Indeed, a feeling of joy would have been a source of guilt, given that in the received wisdom of the teaching that I was subjected to in my youth self-denial and penance paved the way to Heaven.

Indulgences, according to Catholic teaching, meant the remission of punishment in Purgatory, and they could be earned by saying the specified prayers a set number of times. They were a big thing when I was growing up. There were different gradings of indulgences. Partial indulgences meant getting a fixed number of years – like five or ten – knocked off time in Purgatory (which was as bad a place as Hell from a suffering point of view). But it was a temporary state (not like Hell, which was eternal), which is where the indulgences came in. A plenary indulgence was *it* – one could bypass Purgatory altogether and go straight to Heaven. I lost count of the number of plenary indulgences I was sure I earned by saying lots of specified prayers. I only needed one for myself, so I passed on the rest in my prayers to family members and friends and people who I thought were most in need of them. I had a great time saving people from the fires of Purgatory. They didn't know how lucky they were – or maybe the ones who found themselves suddenly transported to Heaven did!

Looking back on all that now, I could find the absurdity of it mildly amusing – if I could ignore the havoc caused in earlier centuries. In those days, indulgences were sold to gullible people in order to encourage them to commit horrendous atrocities against their fellow human beings, with the reward of going straight to Heaven. We need only think of the Inquisition in which so-called heretics were burned at the stake in order to condemn their souls to eternal hellfire, and those who sent them there were promised a direct route to Heaven.

The scenario of indulgences and the type of conditioning that they represented had no place in the philosophy of life being gently outlined to me by my guides. I asked them how was it that there was always such a feeling of joy coming from them. The answer that came through to me, in a humorously direct way, was: *'So you want us to be miserable!'* It was then explained to me that the essence of spirituality is joy, and that the more true we are to ourselves, the more we express joy. And, of course, when we are more truly ourselves, the more centred we are in our own energy, and the more we can help others. If we're miserable we only spread misery.

Strict adherence to any form of conventional thinking, religious or otherwise, causes closed minds. And, as we've already seen, those with closed minds will find it harder to adjust to life in spirit.

The role of religion

I wondered how Monica would take to the notion of reincarnation, which would be entirely at odds with her belief systems, and asked Margaret Anna if she had introduced her to it yet.

Margaret Anna said, *'No, not for a while yet. She needs to be free of her old patterns, particularly to understand that it's OK to enjoy herself, before I go that far. She was always so busy, and felt guilty if she wasn't, that it's very enjoyable for me to see her getting used to doing nothing and coming to the realisation that she's not expected to do anything – or put any pressure on herself in case by being idle she was neglecting her duty. There will be plenty of opportunities for her to serve, if she wants to, as I'm sure she will. Service with a smile!'*

I wanted to know whether there were any people who don't have any 'hang-ups' after they pass on. The encouraging answer was: *'Yes, increasingly so.'*

Margaret Anna explained, *'They're not always easily recognisable when they're on earth, because they don't fit into any pietistic mould or what might be seen as a model of sanctity. If I were to single out a particular feature or characteristic of them it's their open-mindedness. Dogmatism is a no-no for anybody wishing to experience the joy of transition – and I don't mean that in an exclusively religious sense; intolerance in any form fits neatly into its wide embrace.'*

I commented that it might not be a fair question to ask her as the founder of an Order of nuns that's very much alive and well, but I wondered whether the practice of religion was likely to be a hindrance or a help towards experiencing the joy she had mentioned.

I could feel Margaret Anna smiling when she said, *'It's a question that I'd have had to come to sooner or later anyway. It would be strange now if I gave you a dogmatic answer, wouldn't it? I'd be hoist with my own petard, in a manner of speaking.'*

She paused, and then continued, *'Religion is only a tool. It's neither good nor bad – it all depends on how people use it. For many it's a stepping-stone, an introduction to spirituality. People have problems if it becomes the be-all and end-all of spirituality. The more it loses its harshness and rigidity and allows love to take over, the better.'*

I asked her how she thought the Sisters of St Joseph of Peace would react to their founder being involved in disseminating material, much of which is still beyond the pale as far as their Church is concerned.

Margaret Anna replied, *'They shouldn't be surprised. I was a controversial figure as Sister/Mother Francis Clare. Why would I be different now? I was never one to be silenced. I'm speaking to them – and to any others who are open to hearing me – with a message of encouragement, hope and, above all, love. That's a continuing legacy from me. In all humility I can say I'm a conduit of divine love, of which there's an inexhaustible supply. My Sisters are way ahead of the institutional church and have been constantly open to the need to take risks in their thinking and their actions.'*

I asked her whether she had any special message for them now.

She answered: *'Other than that I love and applaud them, no. Each succeeding generation has brought its own dynamism. I'm very grateful that they're no longer ashamed of me! They are idealistic, caring and loving, and are making a big contribution towards peace and harmony on earth.'*

Incidentally, I have met some of the members of the Order both in London and in Dublin. While they showed some surprise that Margaret Anna would choose to communicate with somebody like me – an outsider, so to speak, rather than with one of them – they were most friendly and gracious. Some of them were actively engaged in highlighting Margaret Anna's importance, and the injustices that had been meted out to her. From what I could gather, many of them had entered the Order not knowing that Margaret Anna was the founder. When they found out that she was, it caused at least some of them a lot of confusion. I don't know whether there was scepticism about Margaret Anna being in touch with them or they with her. I thought they were lovely people.

I couldn't resist asking Margaret Anna whether she would still have founded her Order if she had her life as a nun over again, and she gave me a categorical 'yes'.

She said, *'I'm proud of them all, what they are, what they have done and are doing. I've always kept in contact with them – less obsessively since I've lost my bossiness!'*

An exercise in open-mindedness

When we're born our mental processes have not yet swung into action, and as we go through infancy and early childhood, we operate through our feelings. From there, we are naturally influenced by the environment into which we are born, including the cultural, religious, political, traditional and social aspects of our upbringing and the people who surround us. That's how our thinking, the *way* we think, becomes all-important in our approach to life. Do we allow ourselves to be controlled throughout our lives by rigid belief systems carried forward from our childhood and adolescence? Or do we embrace the freedom of being able to examine those belief systems and leave ourselves open to accepting only what makes sense to us?

In my talks and workshops I would usually suggest to participants that they try an experiment when they next found themselves in any form of group discussion. In this type of situation we almost invariably take up immediate positions on the topic under discussion, according to our conditioned way of thinking. I would suggest to the participants that they say nothing at all, but allow themselves to listen without taking up any position on what was being said by the other people in the group. The next step was to observe how they were feeling. Apart from the fact that they might find themselves opening up to different points of view, I hoped that they would begin to feel liberated from the tyranny of fixed positions. That didn't mean, of course, that they wouldn't freely express opinions on anything and everything, but that they would do so in a more tolerant and non-judgemental way.

Everyone, regardless of how they lived their lives on earth, receives guidance and help when they pass on. Their mindsets when they do so can help to make the process that much easier – and, indeed, more enjoyable – or, alternatively, make it difficult for them to experience the pure joy of spirit.

Chapter 8

Looking Forward

I think we can be a lot more comfortable with ourselves if we can accept that we are all spirit beings, who happen to be on a physical adventure on earth with an overall aim of releasing ourselves from conditioned patterns of thinking.

One way in which we are stuck in our thinking is that as humans we feel the need to be able to look forward to tomorrow – we need hope. I asked Margaret Anna whether she ever gets bored, or wishes she had something to look forward to.

She replied, *'Boredom results from restriction of creative expression. I have no such restriction. As regards looking forward, I can if I want to. I can play that sort of game.'*

I wondered what she meant by calling it a game, and she explained that she doesn't need to look forward. She already knows the future because it is all part of the present. However, she can block things if she wants to. As an analogy, say I'm reading a thriller and I don't want to know the ending, I'll make sure not to look at the last pages before I get there.

Margaret Anna acknowledges the need we have to look forward. In exploring this idea, she says, *'It's a truism to say that you can't live in the future any more than you can live in the past. That's why one can say that in real terms there's only the present.'*

She went on to say that if we live in a state of continuing expectancy about the future – the 'I can't wait for such and such to happen' syndrome – we diminish our potential to be able to enjoy the present. We also create a pressure around how we are going to respond to future events when they become our present, because they often fail to live up to expectations. All the same, we wouldn't be human if we didn't feel excitement and a warm glow about the prospect of events that we are anticipating. In fact, in many ways we send that warm glow before us, which prepares the way for our continuing enjoyment of life.

Looking forward positively is likely to create a positive future; however, the opposite is also true. If we're feeling completely miserable about our lives as they are – looking to the future for some event or person to change that situation – we're likely to be disappointed. The way we respond to our present is the way we create our future. That may seem like a hard reality, but it's the recognition of the power of each soul in the exercise of free will. Margaret Anna emphasises that humans have, generally, very little concept of the power of their thoughts, both positive and negative.

Because we as humans exist in a linear time structure of past, present and future, I said that I found it difficult to see how that works in spirit. If souls in spirit exist in a continuing present, is it then a much wider field than ours? Does it encompass what we might call our future?

Margaret Anna replied, *'In other words, can I see your past and your future all rolled into your present? And can I see my own past and my future in my present? I could be clever and say to you that I have no past and no future, and neither have you. But you know that today is Friday and tomorrow is Saturday; the next day is Sunday. This is the month of August, next month is September, and so on. You can't avoid planning ahead, at least to some extent, for tomorrow, next week, next month, next year. I also do forward planning. For example, I prepared strategies in dealing with Johann, Alfredo and Monica. They were loose strategies that could be adjusted spontaneously. I couldn't foresee exactly how they were going to react, although it wasn't difficult to make fairly accurate predictions.'*

What does the future hold?

It's not surprising that many of us are confused about the concept of time in spirit, as well as the idea that events can be predicted. It is, however, an area of huge interest to many people – and I have to confess that it is to me, too. No matter how much I stressed that we're free agents and liable to change our minds about what direction we're taking in our lives, most of the people who came to see me for individual sessions wanted to gain insight into what their future held. They simply didn't want to be told that there's no such thing as the future, merely a continuing present that evolves in line with how open-minded and positive they were in their thinking.

Yes, that's fine, they'd say, but I want to know when I'll meet my soul mate, or get the job I want, or what sorts of careers my children might have (a question I dreaded because there might be as many as seven children involved), or whether a particular venture might be successful, or whether they would always experience good health, or (another question I dreaded) whether the treatment they were having for a health condition would be successful, or how long they would live … and so on and on – the list of potential questions was endless. Of course, it's very natural that these issues will concern us as we journey through life. In fact, on a personal level, I was always delighted when predictions given to me worked out accurately. Sometimes people didn't get the answers they wanted, but with guidance we were often able to find better answers. For example, many of the predictions involved the development of, or changes in, careers. The future isn't set in stone; we all have choices and free will.

So how does it work? Impressions dropped into my mind in response to the questions people asked me. It wouldn't be accurate to say that predictions or, indeed, any communication with the guides came as pictures or words. Instead, I somehow just *knew*. Predictions always involve time, of course, which doesn't feature in spirit because there is only a continuing present. I'm told that souls in spirit are often not any wiser or more advanced than souls temporarily on earth, but that they are in a better position to see the overall picture of happenings on earth. They can, therefore, make more accurate predictions about the future than we can. It's rather like being in a helicopter – or up on top of a mountain – and getting an overall view of what's happening down below. The clarity of the detail depends on how high up the helicopter or the mountain is.

Another analogy that was outlined to me by my guide, Shebaka, involves visualising life on earth as a merry-go-round, with a soul in spirit looking down upon it. It sees what's happening at each stage of the round. For instance, in the case of a person getting on at a particular point, the soul looking down can see the pattern of events that is likely to unfold for that person while he/she stays on the round. The soul can also see what's happening at *all* stages on the round, so it is possible to see the past and future progression on the round. What may seem like a prophecy for someone at point 'X' is really only a description of what's happening at point 'Y', from the point of view of the soul looking down. In other words, no prediction takes place – the soul or spirit guide simply tells us what can be seen a little further along the curve. Of course, if we stop travelling a particular route – by exercising our free will and making different choices – then what the soul has seen may no longer be relevant.

Interestingly, I sometimes found that predictions that were very accurate about *happenings* in a person's life could be widely mistaken about the *timing* of such happenings. When I was new to what are commonly called 'readings' for people, I told a man who had been made redundant from his job that he would get an offer of a type of consultancy role from his former employers. We both assumed that this would be a fairly imminent development. Time passed and nothing happened. Eventually, about two years later, by which time he had long lost faith in the prediction, he did get a consultancy offer from the same firm, which he was glad to accept.

That reading was a good learning experience for me. I began to understand that in spirit everything happens at once, so that the soul making the prediction has to adjust to our linear time scale. Obviously, some souls in spirit become more expert at making that adjustment than others. Frank seems to be a skilled operator in that field.

I can't clearly conceptualise what existence outside time is like. The nearest I can get to it goes something like this. When I'm totally absorbed in a particular activity – such as reading or writing – I have no consciousness of the passage of time. I can be brought back to that consciousness readily enough by, say, being interrupted, but it's suspended temporarily while there are no interruptions. Even though I'm existing in an environment where time features prominently, I'm completely in the present moment.

As I understand it, life in spirit means that we are not limited by consciousness of time, as we are on earth. We can, however, keep up the *illusion* of time to whatever extent we wish, and it is just as real as it is on earth. In a way, that's not really any different from the way things are on earth. For example, until I reached my 40s I don't think I ever really questioned the reality or the existence of time – or, indeed, the planet itself. However, now I see them both as being ultimately illusory. Like my physical body, they are merely transitional features of my evolutionary soul journey. At the same time (!) I have no difficulty in seeing them as 'real' while I'm experiencing them. I can hardly avoid doing so since their (temporary) reality impinges on me in a concrete way every day.

My thoughts often spiralled in different directions when I communicated with Margaret Anna, but, as usual, her comments on anything that entered my thoughts were enlightening. She never minded being interrupted, and her wisdom and understanding provided answers for everything that concerned me at any level.

She continued to answer my questions. *'I can see your past and your future rolled into your present. What was your past in linear terms is obviously clear like history – but recorded more accurately than your histories often are. What will be your future is not so clear in detail, although in broad outline it is. Put in an ultimate setting, we all know where we're going – to complete release from our self-imposed separation from our divine natures. How we get there is influenced by how we exercise our free will.'*

Margaret Anna went on to say, *'Because we agreed that I would act as one of your guides, with your permission I have access to information about all of your evolution, as well as to your overall objectives in reincarnating into your present life. I can see how you have progressed and are progressing in fulfilling what you set out to achieve. In so far as you're staying with your broad plan, I can reasonably expect that you will continue to do so, and therefore I can say with some confidence that I can predict what I would call your future. However, if you decide, or to the extent that you decide, to change course I'll have to change my predictions. I can't interfere with free will, but I can see the patterns in how people exercise their free will and it's not too difficult to foresee what's ahead of them, if I may put it like that.'*

That made complete sense to me. At one stage I used to be curious about other lives I've had, but for a long time now I haven't been. I can always look them up when I move on. Both Margaret Anna and Shebaka have informed me that my involvement in this sort of writing stems from an arrangement made before I was born. Why me, I wondered?

Shebaka said, *'Because this was part of our purpose, I should say is part of our purpose, that you would develop yourself to the stage where it would be possible for me to relay to you some of the wisdom to which I have access. You, in your turn, will find opportunities to pass on this distilled wisdom to others who may be interested.'*

Putting faith in spirit

I commented to Margaret Anna that I assumed that she was talking particularly from the perspective of a guide. What about a soul who is not long in spirit and might still retain controlling tendencies, or want things to happen in a particular way?

Margaret Anna said, *'Yes. A soul in spirit who might not be familiar with all the details of a person's evolution or life purpose could easily allow its own controlling tendencies to take over in giving advice. It might genuinely think it has the person's best interests at heart – and the person might give the advice more weight or see it as infallible as it's coming from a spirit source.*

'At the same time, I don't want to convey an impression that souls in spirit, who are not acting in an agreed arrangement with guides, don't give helpful guidance. I know that they often do. All I'm saying is that it may be a bit "hit and miss". As long as people see it that way and preserve their own power of discrimination, that's fine.

'Can I see my own past and my future in my present? The simple answer is I can with the proviso that I allow myself complete freedom to respond spontaneously to whatever comes up and to express myself in whatever way I wish, without any inhibition or restriction. In other words, I am as I am and in your terms I know I will be as I am.'

In communication with spirits, it's advisable for us to use our own judgement and not always take everything that's said as gospel.

The evolution of life

I wanted to take our consideration of time to another level by exploring the question of life in its continuing evolution. Margaret Anna agreed that it might be interesting for us to look at all that.

She said, *'Suppose we take ourselves as examples. In the physical context, you know where you are at present. You have existed for seventy-six years in your present incarnation on earth. You would describe yourself as being in the closing stages of that incarnation. When the time comes for you to release yourself from your physical body, you hope that you will continue on your voyage of discovery in as open-minded and joyful a way as you can.'*

Margaret Anna explained that she had left the physical dimension behind and, as she had already conveyed to me in an earlier discussion, she didn't propose to sample a further earth existence. She had outlined to me some of the ways in which she experiences her spirit existence – living joyfully and spontaneously, and interacting harmoniously to the best of her ability with all other souls with whom she's in contact. What she regards as an important part of her expression is shining a torch, as it were, to help light the way for souls who are struggling to find themselves.

She asked, *'What lies ahead for me? I don't know and, yet, I do know. An answer not in keeping with my dedication to total simplicity, you might say. I'll elaborate.'*

Margaret Anna said that she knew that she would never again experience death in the same way that I will but she wants to offer comfort for anybody who might be frightened of dying – as many of us are. *'It's tragic that so many humans exist in such states of fear. If by our communications we succeed in eliminating fear from some people's consciousness, we'll have achieved an outcome of immense proportions.'*

How does she know for sure that she will never again experience death? *'I just know it. A sceptic wouldn't consider that an acceptable answer. But it's the best and only answer I can give. The concept of timelessness will help you to understand my answer. The eternal is now and only now. There is no past or future. Consequently, life is ever-continuing.'*

I said to Margaret Anna, 'In my physical state, the past and the future mean a lot to me, although I understand that I can only live in the present. For instance, how can I assess my evolution unless I refer to the past?'

Margaret Anna replied, *'In your earthly evolution your past was a process of physical happenings. Those happenings have faded into the dust of history, with their only surviving importance being the effects they created on your consciousness. When you remember the past, in your terms, you're remembering it in the light of your present consciousness, which is very different from how your consciousness was when the various happenings were taking place. How you are now is the only true reality for you. Do you understand what I'm saying?'*

I answered, 'Yes. In reality, now is all there is because I can only function in my present consciousness.'

Margaret Anna said, *'Death is a feature of time. No time means no death. I am.'*

When souls reincarnate, they move into a situation where time features. They face death in a physical sense again, but, of course, it's only their bodies that die.

Margaret Anna says, *'In accepting that now is all there is and all there can be — since it's not possible to exist in any other state — where does that leave me in terms of increasing awareness? That's what you're wondering about, isn't it? Are there many more walls of understanding that I have to break through before I'm fully realised, so to speak? In order to attempt to explain that to you in human terms, I can say to you that I'm now a vastly more aware being than I was when I was on earth as Margaret Anna.'*

I asked what she meant by 'aware', but she countered by asking me why *I* used that word. After all, I was providing the words for Margaret Anna's communications, as they entered my consciousness.

'It was what came into my head,' I said. 'The sense of what I was receiving from you was to do with your whole range of understanding, freedom and non-judgmentalism, with no more separation from your divine essence.'

'That will do,' said Margaret Anna. *'However, that doesn't mean that I have "arrived". To my knowledge, there's no point of arrival. There's no ultimate destination comprehended in "now". It can only*

imply an infinity of continuity. What that means to me is that I'll be eternally exploring my creative expression joyfully and spontaneously. That's the simplicity of what awaits you, too, and every other soul. How's that?'

'Wonderful,' I said.

Free simply to be

One of the things that Margaret Anna and I are attempting to do in this book is to convey a deeper understanding of how life in spirit connects with physical life and, at the same time, illustrate the similarities and the differences between both dimensions. One of the things that's most intriguing about spirit – and which we, on earth, can often find difficult to grasp – is the question of freedom and, through that, the idea that there can be a complete absence of authority.

I asked Margaret Anna if there were *any* authority figures that she had to obey or, indeed, any rules or laws that prescribe, in even the broadest terms, how celestial societies should function.

Margaret Anna replied, *'I had to put up with enough authority figures in my Margaret Anna life to last me for eternity! No, there's no authority figure at all. Complete and utter freedom. Most people aren't ready for freedom. They seek security in being told what to do or how to be. That's how autocrats and institutions get their power. One of the biggest challenges facing souls is to learn how to be free. Monica is a good example of that.'*

What Margaret Anna is talking about is freedom in the way we think – in other words, being open-minded. I mentioned that I thought it might be difficult for many humans to accept that there is no regulatory system at all in spirit.

As usual, however, Margaret Anna had a reassuring answer. She said, *'There is to the extent that souls, including those temporarily in human form, are being helped to find freedom in themselves. The free spirits, as it were, come together to help those who aren't yet free. It's as simple as that. It's divine love operating through all souls. There can be no boss since we're all equal in God – or, in our divine essence, if you prefer. Some are temporarily at higher levels of awareness than others. That may make them appear to be superior beings, but they know they are not, nor would they want to be. Their objective is to heal rather than increase the suffering caused by some seeking to take precedence over others.'*

As humans, we are so used to hierarchical structures that we find it difficult to imagine life without them. Yet democracy is supposed to be a classless and tolerant form of society that provides equality for all citizens. What Margaret Anna is describing, it seems to me, is democracy in its ideal form – where each soul is free to express its own unique talents and personality, with those who are in a position to do so helping those who still need help.

Margaret Anna explained to me that she didn't need help herself because she's gone past that stage. *'As I mentioned earlier, we tend to operate in groups or committees – if we wish to do so, of course. We have lots of discussions. We're always available to each other. I don't really need help. I don't mean to sound arrogantly self-sufficient, but since you've asked the question I'm answering it as honestly as I can. I don't have any material needs. I exist spontaneously and I can do so in ways that would be difficult for humans because of all the restrictions with which they have to cope. You see, souls need help while they're still separated from their divinity. Separation equals helplessness.'*

I asked her whether there was any basis for fear that unity with divinity (or a Source or God) might, perhaps, lead to a loss of individuality?

Margaret Anna replied, *'None at all. Unity means a totally free flow of divine energy within each soul and enables each soul to be fully itself in every way.'*

When I see my question as meaning unity with unconditional love, I have no difficulty in conceptualising her answer.

Continuing in spirit

I asked Margaret Anna what would happen if she decided that she was tired of being a guide. Would she get fed up because souls, both in human form and in spirit, didn't seem to be getting anywhere despite her attempts to help them?

She replied, *'You're asking me to suppose something that couldn't happen. I don't get tired and I don't get fed up either. It's easy for me because I don't exist within limitation. And I know that there's always a way to achieve a breakthrough, as with Alfredo. I can wait, you see*

— I don't have a deadline, if you'll excuse the pun! As some stage I may discontinue acting as a guide in the way that I do at present. Eventually I will anyway, as no one will need my help.'

I said that I assumed that this was a long way off.

Margaret Anna said, '*Yes, indeed, unfortunately.'*

There must be areas or dimensions of which Margaret Anna had little or no knowledge, I countered. How could she help everyone?

She said, '*There are myriad projects — dimensions of experience — that hold no interest for me. I only delve into whatever interests me. I can find out about other matters if somebody asks me, or if I want to, at any particular stage. Let's say that l know where to get my answers, whenever I need them. I don't carry all the knowledge of the universe around in my head, if that's what you're asking. I can consult my celestial internet whenever I like! I can be as deliberately ignorant or deliberately knowledgeable as I want to be.'*

I'd felt comfortable chatting to Margaret Anna from the start, but as we got to know each other better I realised there were no barriers to our communication at all. There was nothing I couldn't ask her if I wanted to. I was long past the stage of being amazed to find that I was in communication with a nineteenth-century nun, but she still sometimes surprised me with her humour and irreverence, as well as her profound wisdom. I felt, and still feel, very lucky to be in contact with her in this way and, through her, to have some access to that celestial internet she talks about.

Learning acceptance

Back on earth we have a long way to go to accept that we have to take some things on trust rather than trying to look forward and know all the answers. This was often a problem for me when I gave readings. I mentioned earlier that I tried to avoid situations in which people would come to me specifically to get messages from 'dead' relatives or friends. If they told me that beforehand, in the early days in particular, my immediate inclination was to refuse to see them. If I did relent and allow them to come, I would always warn them that I couldn't guarantee that the relatives in question would be ready to come through. It was also possible that they would not find me a compatible agent through which to communicate. In any case, I always asked my guides (including Margaret Anna, of course) for help.

One day a woman named Lorraine came to see me. Her mother, Geraldine, who had passed away some years previously, came through. It was one of the most fluent communications I ever experienced. Geraldine gave all sorts of (totally accurate) information about Lorraine's life and family, and provided advice that Lorraine found very helpful. As usual, I can't remember the details of the advice, but I do remember the overall expression of satisfaction with the reading – both on my part and on Lorraine's.

Naturally enough, I suppose, Lorraine's sister Kim wanted to pay a visit, too. With my usual warning, I agreed. We got plenty of information from her guides, but there was no sign of Geraldine. Even though Geraldine had given Kim lots of messages through Lorraine, Kim desperately wanted the direct experience and she was most disappointed. So was I, but there was nothing I could do about it. In my earlier experience with Lorraine, Geraldine had come across to me as very loving. However, she obviously had her own reasons for coming through directly to one daughter and not to the other. Maybe she felt that she had already transmitted enough information, and that Kim needed to trust more. I couldn't throw any more light on the subject. I had to accept that that was the way it was meant to be on that occasion. Perhaps she would have a later experience where Geraldine would come through to her.

On another day a woman named Rose called me to tell me that her mother, Cynthia, had recently passed away and that she was desperate to hear from her. I tried to persuade her not to come, using every argument I could think of, but she kept pleading with me until I eventually gave in. She arrived full of expectancy. I consulted with my guides and, through them, Rose's guides, and I poured out whatever information was coming to me about her and her life. But nothing came from Cynthia. I could sense that Rose was getting more and more exasperated. Somebody in the house where I was giving the reading opened the door and asked if we would like any sandwiches. It's worth noting that this sort of interruption had never occurred before – and wouldn't normally in those situations. It was probably an angel in disguise! That was the last straw for Rose. She jumped up from her chair and left in high dudgeon.

I could laugh about that experience afterwards, but it took me quite a while to shake off the effects of it – the feelings of embarrassment and disappointment, and questioning myself about why I ever got involved in doing that sort of work. But it soon became clear to me that that experience – and the experience with Kim – affirmed the validity and the honesty of how communication between the dimensions was working for me.

Both incidents reinforce what I said earlier about 'trying'. I wanted to fulfil the expectations of Kim and Rose because I knew precisely what those expectations were. Just as I'd found that my talks were most effective when I stood up and spoke spontaneously off the top of my head, so it is with readings. Things always worked out so much better for me when I was able to go along with the free flow of whatever was coming to me, without letting myself be persuaded to try to get answers to specific questions. The human need to look forward, while perhaps understandable, is not part of the natural way of spirits.

Chapter 9

A Place of Our Own

One of the most basic needs that we have as human beings is a place to live – ideally, a place of our own, either alone or with loved ones, where we can have our personal possessions and lifestyle. The prospect of giving up all of our material trappings and entering a sort of communal timelessness sounds rather daunting.

I mentioned earlier, however, that Margaret Anna told me all she had to do was think of something and it manifested. I had previously been informed that this was the way things worked in spirit.

As we humans are not yet able to wish up our ideal homes, I thought that this might be a subject worth exploring further with Margaret Anna.

She said, *'Your residences are solid structures that are usually fixed in one place and not transportable. We can create any type of building we like just by imagining it. And if, after a while, we don't like what we've got, we may wish to transform it or have something totally different. We can have instant manifestation, according to our wishes. Many souls who have been house-proud on earth find to their great joy that they can create exact replicas of what they left behind – just by thinking about them. Or keen gardeners can, as it were, transport their gardens (not physically, of course) to their new surroundings. These are not flimsy cardboard cut-out structures. They're just as "real" as yours, although that's difficult for you to conceptualise. The same thing applies to food and drink – or anything that's available on earth. We can have the experience of them in whatever way we wish, once we realise we can.'*

It's actually not so difficult for me to conceptualise what she was talking about. Even in our physical world the only way creation happens is, initially, through the mind. For example, if I paint a picture, write a book, make a chair – or anything at all – it happens through my thoughts. The actual creation doesn't exist in physical terms until I do something resulting from a thought. Creation is, quite simply, a manifestation of my thoughts.

In fact, what we describe as creation – a building, say – would never have existed unless somebody first designed it mentally. It started as a *thought*. The same situation exists in spirit, except that there's no physical labour involved in putting the design into effect. This makes life a lot easier for those of us who don't enjoy physical work – although that can be added into the package, if we so wish.

I said to Margaret Anna that, in my understanding, a big difference between life in spirit and life on earth is that the soul in spirit can have the home that suits its style at any given time. On earth, of course, the poor human can only have what he or she can afford.

Margaret Anna added, *'You can throw in, too, that the soul in spirit doesn't have to cope with ageing or physical illness or disability of any kind. It seems a bit unfair, doesn't it?'*

When I replied, 'Just a bit!', Margaret Anna continued.

'Remember, though, that souls choose to incarnate or reincarnate into the physical world. There's no compulsion whatever on them to do so. As you know, their choice is influenced by their need to free themselves from patterns that they had established during previous earth experiences. The quickest way to do that is likely to be re-entering similar types of environment that would confront them with those patterns.

'I wouldn't like to give an impression that life on earth is intended to be a very serious, gloomy sort of ironing-out experience. I know that that has been a common view of it, but happily it's changing.'

Traditional church teachings of old used to be that life is a vale of tears, but now a more positive belief is commonplace that life on earth is to be enjoyed rather than seen as a penance.

Sex and procreation

If having a home is one of our most basic needs as a human being – a need that is amply met in spirit – it would be interesting to examine whether the other needs that define our time on earth are equally met. For example, much of our time on earth is driven by sex and by money. Margaret Anna had already made it abundantly clear that we have no need for money in spirit, but what about sex? What about having babies?

Margaret Anna provided a clear answer: *'How could it be that something to which so much energy is devoted on earth would not feature powerfully in spirit? Money is in a different category from sex; while it is, of course, a form of energy or exchange of energy, it's external to people – something they use, like furniture or washing machines. Sex, on the other hand, is a deeply intimate form of communication between people. We know that it's commercialised and abused, but that doesn't take away from its beauty in its ideal usage.*

'As you have often seen, when people expand their awareness, they are no longer satisfied with sexual relations, per se; rather they're looking for soul mates with whom they can enjoy sexual intimacy as a special form of communication – a profoundly spiritual experience. It happens that people don't meet soul mates in a particular lifetime or, if they do, circumstances prevent them from getting together. The resultant loneliness and longing can be devastating for some; others are happy with special friendships that don't have sexual overtones.

'The good news is that all souls have soul mates. They find them sooner or later, and get together with them in a total sharing, which includes sexual intimacy, if they so wish.'

Then, of course, there was a question of babies. I had met many women who desperately wanted to have children of their own. That's something that hadn't featured nearly as much – in fact, hardly at all – in my sessions with men. I don't mean to imply that men don't want children – I know many do – but I'm just recording my own experience. If it is, however, an over-whelming desire for women to bear children – and perhaps something that was not satisfied on earth – would it occur in spirit?

Margaret Anna confirms, *'Don't I keep telling you that every-thing is possible in spirit? The whole panoply of earth was set up from spirit. All your miracles are engineered in spirit. There are no new souls, just souls taking on different forms. Thus, with your babies. So, of course, babies can be born in spirit, if souls so wish. Souls can even experience all the joys of childbirth if they want to do so. Just bear in mind that anything that's possible on earth is, countless times, more easily achieved in spirit.'*

So, I pondered, 'A woman who, say, suffered deep disappoint-ment by not having her longing for a baby satisfied on earth can look forward to having her dream realised in spirit?'

Margaret Anna replied, *'Indeed she can.'*

Be careful what you wish for

Making a wish in spirit is immediately fulfilled, but what about wishes on earth? I used to tell the following story at some of my talks.

On the day of their 60th birthdays, a married couple who shared the same birth date were having breakfast when an angel suddenly appeared beside the table. The angel said to them that, in order to celebrate such important birthdays, they could each have one wish.

After her initial surprise, the wife said that she'd make her wish.

'You know,' she said, 'I have always wanted to have a nice conservatory where I could sit and relax and let the world go by, but we could never afford it.'

'Is that your wish?' asked the angel.

'Yes', she answered without hesitation.

She looked out and there, before her eyes, was the most beautiful conservatory she'd ever seen. She jumped up and down with joy.

Then the angel turned to her husband. He moved closer to the angel, out of earshot of his wife, who, in any case, was completely preoccupied with her new conservatory.

'What's your wish?' asked the angel.

Out of the corner of his mouth, he said, ' I'd like to have a woman twenty years younger than me.'

'Are you quite sure?' asked the angel.

'Oh yes,' he replied firmly.

Then, instantly, he was 80.

If he was in spirit, he could have cancelled his wish. Since he was still on earth, he couldn't. Maybe we're lucky that we don't always get what we wish for.

Spacelessness

I think that maybe it's easy (and certainly nice) to imagine the prospect of having anything and everything we want and need – our deepest desires fulfilled – in spirit. It is, perhaps, the overall quality of spirit that's more difficult to grasp. In particular, I think it's very difficult for us to conceptualise the idea of there being no such thing as *space* in spirit. We are concerned with space in all aspects of the way we live. Our fields, roads, cars, houses, shops, buses, trains, aeroplanes and, of course, our bodies take up space. Everything that we know has a boundary of some kind. In fact, in the human condition we can be confused by a lack of boundaries, which induce in us a comfortable familiarity.

The nearest I have come to understanding the concept of spacelessness is when I heard about YouTube. It seems that YouTube is endless. Videos and everything else can be continuously uploaded, and nobody shouts 'Stop! We're out of space.' When we talk, the sounds that issue from our mouths don't take up any space, unless we write them down or record them in some way. The words go off on a journey that's not confined by any boundaries. It would be impossible, I think, to try to imagine the amount of space that would be needed to contain all of the words that we pour forth – not to mention what we'd need if we were to throw in our thoughts as well!

While I was struggling with the concept of solid structures and yet no space in spirit, I thought it would be a good idea to ask my friend Frank how he came to terms with the apparent contradictions between the two ideas. His transition from the physical to the spirit dimension had been comparatively recent, but still long enough ago for him to have become familiar with his present situation.

As usual, he was most accommodating. Frank said he realised that he was dead immediately because he was looking down at his body. He felt what he could only describe as a 'lightness', as if a great weight had been lifted off him. Even though I am slightly hesitant to include this, he wanted to stress that his familiarity with my writings helped him to make a transition. Why? Because he knew what to expect. He was met and cosseted, and made to feel that he was the most important being in the universe. Although I digress here, I did want to make it clear that having an understanding – and almost a prior acceptance – of what is to come makes it that much easier to embrace the spacelessness that comprises spirit.

Frank said that the best way he could answer my questions, he thought, was to address them from a personal rather than a general point of view. He told me about the group with which he's associated, and how they try to help newly arrived souls feel at home. They get together as and when they feel like doing so, and they have lots of fun.

Frank said, *'What you're interested in, though, at present is what I might call the mechanics of all that – such as, do we have a special room or building where we meet? Is the room in a fixed location? Does it have furniture? Do we sit down or stand up?'*

He answered this by saying that anything is possible. However, he continued that despite how well prepared he was when he arrived, he still had a lot of adjustments to make. The biggest surprise he got was how immediately thoughts were actualised. When Frank was on earth, he might say (in a vague sort of way) something like, 'I wish I had a nice car instead of the old banger I have.' He'd say this in the full knowledge that nothing would happen. However, in spirit, if he were to express a wish like that, a new car would appear in front of him. He'd have to cancel the wish, of course, as he has no need of cars in spirit.

Frank said, *'As you're writing this, you're sitting in an armchair. As I'm whispering in your ear, as it were, I'm also sitting in an armchair. You're saying to yourself that your armchair is taking up a measurable amount of space in a room, but you can't grasp how my armchair isn't taking up space similarly. I could say to you – like the woman in the bus did – "You'll find out soon enough." But I'll have mercy on you and I won't!'*

So, what did Frank mean? He said that, very simply, thought equals creation – that all creation is a product of thought. All he needed to do was to imagine himself sitting in an armchair similar to mine – and as solid as mine – and immediately he was. He understood that I was still stuck with the dilemma of trying to understand how his armchair isn't occupying space.

Ultimately, the best answer he could give me was that all space is an illusion – temporarily created in order to confine souls in physical bodies and within physical boundaries so that they'd have to face themselves and be helped to find freedom in their thoughts. But Frank wasn't getting into that. *'It has been explained to you by more advanced souls than I am,'* he said.

I think that, with typical modesty, he was playing down his own level of advancement.

Frank asked me to suppose that as I'm sitting in my armchair my body is a solid structure that occupies space. When my body eventually 'gives up the ghost' – *'an interesting description, don't you think?'* – it will be cremated, as is my wish, and will become virtually spaceless. Even my body is moving out of space into spacelessness, so to speak. When we leave this earth, we leave our bodies behind. We leave behind the part of us that occupies space. Frank explained that my body, as it is now, is merely an illusion – a temporary illusion while I am on earth. When I leave this earth I'll be able to move into my spirit body – with all its pristine glory – and it will be as solid to me as it is now. It won't even take up as much space as its ashes; in reality, no space at all.

Frank went on to say, *'I have given you a very rough analogy, but maybe you can settle for it. I'd have to have you here with me to help you understand completely, but I don't think you're quite ready for that yet! In the end, the best answer of all that I can give is to repeat what you've already been told. That is, everything is possible in spirit. I'm still finding that out.'*

My heart was warmed by his next message. Frank said, *'Our entire group send loving greetings from "outer spacelessness", to all our "spaced-out" friends on earth, including all those who may be drawn to reading your book.'*

Developing communication

The constant development of technology seems to be moving us towards understanding the concept of spacelessness. When I started work we didn't even have photocopiers. Eventually we acquired computers, which have continued to be designed to make ever-decreasing demands on space. And I don't think I'll ever get over the wonder of mobile phones. (Not that I use them all that much – I can't even do texting.) Imagine being able to stand in the middle of a field in Ireland and telephone somebody in Australia! I'm selecting Australia deliberately, as it's commonly referred to as being 'down under' in the same way as we allude to spirit dimensions as being 'above' and earth as 'below'. When I was young, I – and I'm sure most, if not all, of my contemporaries – would have thought of a mobile phone as something that was utterly inconceivable. Certainly, if I could have conceived of it, I'd have regarded it as a miracle.

It's obvious that there will be no stopping the development of technology. My vision, using the example of speaking to somebody 'down under' by mobile phone, is that communication between the spirit and physical dimensions will become as commonplace as that between people at different ends of the earth. We on earth will be 'down under', in a manner of speaking, and our spirit friends will be 'up above' – using a link like a mobile phone that will be able to transmit thoughts in an easier way than telepathy. There won't be any mystique about that sort of communication and it will certainly make more obvious the fact that there are no goodbyes in any permanent sense.

While I am waiting for my vision to take effect, as it's unlikely to happen in my lifetime (Margaret Anna didn't enlighten me on that – I didn't want her to, really), I thought that in my attempts to get deeper understanding of conditions in spirit it would be informative if I concentrated on Margaret Anna herself in the context of what she might want personally; for example, whether she had a place of her own.

As usual, Margaret Anna was a step ahead of me, having already known that I was thinking along those lines. She deliberately generalised my thought. It wasn't that she didn't want to answer my questions, or provide insight into her own life in spirit; she thought it was more important to paint the general picture for me before dwelling on her personal situation.

She said that there's a gradualism that operates in spirit as well as on earth. It's to do with expansion of consciousness or awareness. At one stage in her evolution she'd have accepted that having a house or an apartment of her choice was a more or less fixed reality – as she would similarly have done on earth.

But, as her awareness expanded, she became more and more open to the true nature of reality – which is that she's continually creating it from within herself. In other words, there's nothing stagnant or fixed where she's concerned.

During her adulthood, in her last life on earth as Margaret Anna, her home was a movable feast. She never really had a place that she could call her own. In the long run, that was an advantage for her – and she wanted to stress that she was only talking about herself here – because she wasn't married to any particular building or locality, although there were times when she'd like to have been.

I enquired whether she was saying that she didn't have any particular home now, but she wanted to explore that question further with me. Suppose, she suggested, I had the freedom to be instantly wherever I'd like to be – by myself or with whomever I wished to be; out in the open, or ensconced in the most comfortable surroundings I could imagine – would I confine myself to one fixed setting?

She continued, *'If, in your present environment or circumstances, you say "no", you might regard yourself as taking an easy way of escaping from your responsibilities – or creating difficulties for yourself, by having to adapt to different cultures, including methods of entertainment, such as television programmes. But suppose you have no responsibilities. Yes, you want to help others but you're not going to be of any use to them if you get all caught up in their troubles. The best way you can help them is to guide them towards taking responsibility for* themselves. You would be in a position to do that in spirit. There are no different cultures, as that's a feature of life on earth only. In spirit you could see any television programme you wanted, if you were still interested.'

She went on, 'Now, may I put the question to you again. In that scenario would you confine yourself to one setting?'

'No,' I answered.

Margaret Anna continued, 'That's my answer. I don't mean to imply that what suits me, suits any others. What I'm talking about is being free, free to be, from which follows freedom to do whatever one chooses to do. Being free in myself means that I allow that freedom to each and every soul. This in turn means that there's no question of trying to control any of them. Freedom also means loving. Once I'm free in myself I'm free to love unconditionally; I will only attach conditions to my loving if I'm feeling confined or insecure in myself.'

I wanted to know how different she was now from how she had been when she was last on earth as Margaret Anna.

She replied: 'You know how blinkers are sometimes put on a horse to prevent it from looking sideways in horseracing? The horse can only see straight ahead. I was blinkered when I was on earth – deliberately so, in order to fulfil my purpose there. I was like the racehorse. I could only see what was directly in front of me, and my concentration was focused on that. When I moved back to life in spirit, after I had adjusted to it, I could see how my role slotted into the panorama of evolution – the grand design of life, if you like.

'I'm very different, and I'm not different at all – which are seemingly contradictory statements, but yet both true. Each soul has basic *qualities – or perhaps style would be a better description – which are constant, although often partially or nearly totally obscured. The big difference now is that I'm free, with all that that means. I obviously wasn't free while I was on earth.'*

It's nice to know that when we move on to the spirit world we can continue to enjoy all the comforts and activities that we do on earth – and more besides – without any of the hardships.

Chapter 10

Earthbound Souls

The ability to achieve our dreams and have our wishes fulfilled is a comforting – even exciting – prospect for most of us. In spirit we will have the ability to harness the power of our thoughts and make our dreams a reality. However, when souls don't realise the power of their thoughts their ability to live joyfully in spirit can be undermined.

There are, for example, some souls who can't or won't let go of earth – souls who resent finding themselves in their new state. Margaret Anna explained to me that these include people who were serious users (or abusers) of alcohol or drugs, who lived much of their lives in public houses or the like (which they continue to frequent after the death of their bodies). People who were so attached to their houses and possessions that they cannot bear to tear themselves away also find it difficult to move on to spirit. So, too, do people who built their lives around their businesses and cannot believe that others could be capable of managing them; these souls stick around to keep an eye on them. Sooner or later, of course, guides find a way to prise them loose.

It occurred to me that it might, therefore, be a serious disadvantage for people to become very attached to material possessions, or earthly belongings or pleasures, such as a house or a garden. Margaret Anna agreed that it could be detrimental to do so, although the effect is dependent upon the level of attachment. She notes that if we are obsessive about our homes to the extent that they are the predominating feature in our lives, this will slow down our progress in spirit. Interestingly, it seems that some souls can become as obsessed with their spirit houses as they were with their earthly homes. In either case, obsessions about anything – from lifestyle, business and relationships, to homes and material possessions – should be avoided, as they sidetrack the soul's journey towards increased awareness.

'Earthbound' is an appropriate description for souls who, for one reason or another, don't want to move away from their familiar surroundings. In my experience, that sometimes happens because souls don't realise, or don't want to accept, that they're 'dead'. For example, those who didn't believe in continuing life would find it hard to accept that they weren't still alive in the physical sense.

One night, some time ago, I woke suddenly and felt a presence in the corner of the bedroom. This was a soul that had defiantly refused to accept that he was no longer in his physical body. I had never met him when he was alive on earth, but

I heard that he had died suddenly. In spite of all the evidence around him, which included people neither hearing nor seeing him (or, indeed, being aware of him in any shape or form), he was stubbornly refusing to accept that he was dead.

This man visited me several times until one night, when I wanted to go back to sleep, I gently suggested that he should look for a light that would guide him to a more joyful life than he had previously experienced. My guides had told me that this was a way of helping earthbound souls to accept their new state. I don't know what he did because I fell asleep again and he was gone when I woke up.

I have met quite a few people who have seen or felt spirits around them, and have been terrified by the experience. There was no need for them to be afraid, of course. Usually the souls were only visiting to express their love or to give confirmation of life after death. In some cases they may simply have been feeling confused or depressed, and found it difficult to let go of familiar surroundings or people.

In the early stages of my communication with guides I asked them not to allow any souls to come through to me except by mutual agreement. It's like having an alarm system installed in my aura. I have only asked once; there was no need to keep asking. Now I know that, if I feel there's a soul near me, my guides consider that the contact is helpful – either for the soul, or somebody connected with it, or me, or all of us. After that, I'm open to whatever form the communication takes.

In a course I was running some years ago, a participant named Gary noticed that there was a small boy standing near him. He could describe the boy in precise detail. At the same time Gary experienced a headache that refused to go away. The boy was looking all around him, as if he didn't know where he was or what to do. I thought he might have been killed in an accident or something like that. I suggested to Gary that when he next saw the boy he might convey to him through his thoughts that he would see a light coming towards him. This light would be an angel coming for him, who would love and mind him, and the boy should go with the angel. At the next meeting Gary told us that he did that. He saw the light coming towards the boy, who held out his hand and left with what Gary presumed was an angel. His headache disappeared at exactly the same time.

It might be logical to ask why the guide didn't come to the boy directly, without involving Gary and, incidentally, the rest of the participants on the course. However, the way it was done gave marvellous affirmation and encouragement to all of us and we had the great joy of knowing that the little boy was happily adjusting to his new state. The incident gave us a good example of how to help souls in a very simple way. Gary's headache might have been due to the stress caused by his empathy with the boy's distress but it provided a physical proof to him that he wasn't hallucinating.

Fear of the paranormal

In my experience over the past thirty years or so I have found that the paranormal or supernatural forms the basis of one of the most common sources of fear. I realise, of course, that because I have been existing in a sort of 'in-between' world for many years, the people with whom I have had the most contact will have tended to gravitate towards that world. However, interest in the 'after world' and the supernatural has been increasing at a hugely accelerating rate in recent years, and I thought it would be helpful to share some of my experiences so that any who may be hovering on the edge of further exploration might understand that there's nothing to fear. Once fear of death – and all that goes with it – is taken out of the reckoning, other fears, multi-faceted though they can be, lose their power.

My understanding is that there's no reason whatever for us to be afraid of a spirit causing us harm. Sources of physical danger are confined to the physical world. That's enough for us to have to contend with without having to worry about invisible entities attacking us.

I felt that it would be helpful to explore the subject of earthbound souls further with Margaret Anna. It's obviously a hugely important feature in the relationship between life on earth and life in spirit.

Margaret Anna has reiterated (and continues to do so) that what we call 'death' is, in effect, simply change – a movement from one dimension to another. People know that they're going to die at some stage, in the physical sense, but for various reasons they do everything in their power to keep at bay what they perceive to be the 'evil day'. And, even when that day comes, as it inevitably does, many continue to believe, and often succeed in convincing themselves, that they're still alive on earth, in spite of the fact that, frustratingly, their friends and relatives don't think so and don't acknowledge them when they try talking to them. But they don't give up easily. They want to continue to be part of what they were used to. They may attach themselves to a familiar building or an armchair within it; they may cling to a person – usually someone who is continuing to grieve for them. In our terms, this may go on for many years – in spite of all the efforts of their guardian angels and friends in spirit who want to help them to adjust to their new situation.

Margaret Anna said that she would like to explain her views about how humans can most effectively help those souls who continue to remain earthbound after they have left their physical bodies.

She explained, *'Religious practice would tend to encourage devotional exercises, such as prayers, novenas, memorial services, etc. I have the utmost sympathy for humans. I know what I'm talking about since I was one myself. They're in the unfortunate position that they're scrambling around in the dark, in a manner of speaking. They can't see the rounded, bigger picture in the way we in spirit can. If they could, they would soon see that all their prayers, etc., only succeed in making* themselves *feel better. If you think about it, isn't it obvious that it's a redundant exercise to pray to God on behalf of somebody? The flow of unconditional love embraces every soul and can't be more than it is, since it's infinite. The only barrier to its fullest expression in each individual is the receptivity of the individual to allow that expression. To the earthbound soul who doesn't want to "move on", devotional exercise on his/her behalf can only be a source of agitation and rejection. I know now that the traditional rituals to which I myself subscribed when I was on earth are, at best, ineffective as a source of help to earthbound souls and, at worst, counterproductive.'*

That may go against everything we have understood to be true. But what exactly is prayer intended to do for the deceased? Are we asking God – as the ultimate judge – to treat the departed soul with mercy and forgiveness? Well, since there isn't a judgmental God, this type of prayer is a futile exercise. If, however, prayers are offered as a way of sending unconditionally loving thoughts to the departed souls – or asking our guides to convey our love to them and help them in whatever ways they may need to be helped – then that's a different story. In that way, we're assured that prayer can most definitely be effective.

According to my guides, the best way of helping souls – in both their physical bodies *and* spirit – is by doing an exercise, such as the one outlined in Chapter 4, which involves imagining ourselves in a circle with our guides, linking in with the unconditional love of the universe (God) and uniting ourselves with that love as it flows around the souls.

I couldn't help but ask Margaret Anna whether many people would reject this idea out of hand, simply because it goes against the huge accumulation of religious teachings. Wouldn't some people consider it sacrilegious?

Margaret Anna said, *'So they would.'*

'Years ago,' I said, 'I'd have thought so myself, when I was earnestly on the quest for indulgences for the suffering souls in Purgatory. There wasn't any hope for the souls in "limbo", so there was no point in wasting prayers on them.'

Margaret Anna agreed, saying, *'And now there's no limbo in revised church teaching! So, you see, things change even within the most rigid institutional frameworks. In my own sojourn as Sister/Mother Francis Clare, I eventually found the inflexible patriarchal authoritarianism of my hierarchical superiors intolerable – and for this I was condemned as an apostate. Change has infiltrated there, too, and produced a softening of attitudes. When you were growing up you were taught that nobody could be saved outside of the "one true Church". That, too, has changed. We're aiming to move the process of change further along in so far as we can. People need to challenge their belief systems and determine how they really feel about them.'*

Helping earthbound souls

So, how can we help earthbound souls effectively? Margaret Anna has been witness to many cases of souls who have found it difficult to make the transition to spirit, and she has suggested ways in which they can be guided to the light.

She noted that it's important that we remind ourselves that people who are obsessive as humans will still be obsessive when they move out of the physical state – unless they can find freedom in the way they think. Spirit guides help them to achieve that freedom.

Margaret Anna reminded me of the story of Alfredo, the criminal gang leader. He wanted to continue as he had been on earth, and couldn't accept that he was no longer in his physical body. He was so obsessed with his need to control his minions and his empire that, despite their best efforts, the guides couldn't get through to him. It wasn't until they arranged to have his childhood friend, Lucilla, appear to him as she had been when they were both children that his obsessive barriers were broken down to the extent that he would allow himself to be helped.

Margaret Anna explained that one of the many wonderful things that are happening at present is the vastly increased (and increasing) level of cooperation between the physical and spirit worlds. That has been a direct result of the breakdown of institutional frameworks, with their emphasis on adherence to prescribed ways of thinking. Now more and more people do not fear the spirit world in the way previous generations did. Once fear is removed, there's no limit to the possibilities.

Guides are, of course, continually helping earthbound souls, and they do so in many ways. But, as far as the guides are concerned, the process of getting through to those souls is generally far too long. One way in which the process can be speeded up is to accept the help of the souls who are, at present, in physical form. Why? Because earthbound souls still exist in the dense atmosphere of earth; they are drawn to it, as if magnetised. Therefore others who share that atmosphere – and who are consciously in a cooperative arrangement with guides – can act as conduits for the earthbound souls.

Margaret Anna outlined a good illustration of this in practice. She asked me to imagine that I am a gambler. I spend a lot of time every day studying racing form and placing bets. Sometimes I win, but more often I lose. I'm in the grip of an obsessive pattern of behaviour that I don't wish to change. But, unfortunately in my view, change is forced upon me, as I succumb to a heart attack. There's a lot of commotion around me; people are talking about me, and saying things like 'such a nice man, what a pity he had the misfortune to fall into the grip of a gambling habit'. Some of the comments are charitable; others condemn my irresponsibility in wasting money at the expense of my family. I try talking to some of the people – members of my family and friends – but they ignore me. Even though I plant myself in front of them, they look through me as if I'm not there.

I urgently need to find out which horse won the last race. I rush to the bookmaker's office, where I see some of the regulars like myself. I ask them who won the race. All of them seem to have gone deaf and blind. I don't exist, as far as they're concerned.

What can I do? People are talking about me as if I'm dead. But I know I'm not dead. I'm still the same person as I always was. My life, at least the latter part of it, has revolved around gambling – studying the racing pages of newspapers, placing bets, waiting for results and, when I'm lucky, collecting winnings. That's what I want to continue to do and all my attention is concentrated on getting things back to the way they were.

Needless to say, my guides are constantly monitoring my progress or, more accurately, lack of it. They know that they'll have to be patient as they attempt to divert me from my obsession. Because I'm still firmly attached to the earth's atmosphere, I can't see them when they come near me. They know they'll succeed in getting my attention eventually, but they would dearly love to make an early breakthrough.

It so happens that I have a friend who misses me very much, even though I haven't seen a lot of him since my gambling addiction took hold of me. I'm drawn to stay around him when the bookmaker's office is closed, in the hope that he'll acknowledge my presence. But he doesn't.

One evening I go with him as he visits a house. At this house he is ushered in by a woman, who almost immediately starts talking about me – and how she saw me coming in the door with him. She obviously sees me or senses my presence. Now she's talking to me and asking me questions. It's as if I'm on some sort of a wavelength with her. She passes on my answers to my friend. He's very moved by the whole process. I'm also moved and relieved that, at last, I'm able to get through to someone.

Now the woman is suggesting to me that it would be good for me to move on, that there are many friends in spirit who want to help me adjust to my changed situation. I'm a bit doubtful about that idea, but she assures me that I'll still be able to contact my friend or anybody else I might wish to contact. She suggests to me that I should look for a light that will, seemingly, beckon me to go towards it. If I do, she says, I'll find that a wonderfully loving guide will be there to take my hand and lead me towards all those who are waiting to give me a big welcome. I'm tired of feeling isolated and I agree to go, much to my relief when I discover what's waiting for me.

Margaret Anna said that she couldn't over-emphasise the value of the marvellous work being done by those commonly – but inadequately – known as 'mediums' or 'channels'. Those people not only help souls to release themselves from earthbound conditions, but they provide comfort for grieving relatives and friends who are open-minded enough to allow themselves to be helped in that way. It's important to stress, however, that this work is ideally done in close cooperation with the humans' spirit guides, although, of course, people can talk directly to loved ones without guides. Once they accept the notion that it is possible, all they have to do is send out thoughts and they will be picked up.

Accelerating the process

Margaret Anna is very clear about the fact that the ability to help earthbound souls is not confined to any one category of people. The main requirements are open-mindedness and motivation to help. From the guides' point of view, a highly effective way of accelerating the process of helping these souls is the creation of small groups of open-minded, non-judgemental people getting together periodically, setting up a cooperative link with their guides and lending their physicality towards attracting earthbound souls into a situation where they are likely to be receptive to receiving help.

Margaret Anna wasn't talking about séances, which suggest a more formal type of setting. In fact, what she means is something quite different – using the combined energy of open-minded people to reach souls who need help.

She explained that when a few people who are on similar wavelengths get together in a common purpose – and when they combine in that purpose with their guides – she couldn't adequately convey to me how powerful the effect is. Guides operate on both individual and group bases. The group has an advantage in that it provides companionship, support and affirmation. In a physical context, the group places fewer demands on each individual member. Earthbound spirits can draw on your energy, leaving you physically tired and sometimes causing a depressed mood, in much the same way as a negative person on earth can pull you down, but with a group there is more energy to go around. On the other hand, the individual operating on his/her own doesn't have to make special arrangements about travel, timing, etc., and this can be an advantage. In any case, what would usually happen is that any helpfully motivated person would find opportunities to cooperate with his/her guides on both an individual and a group basis. In the spirit dimension there are obviously no physical demands. In any given situation Margaret Anna can operate spontaneously in whatever way seems best.

A group of four of us met regularly for about two years for the specific purpose of helping earthbound souls. We had a special arrangement with a guide, whom we knew as Lucius. He acted as a sort of master of ceremonies. Through the good offices of Lucius, we were able to make contact with quite a number of souls that hadn't moved on from the earth's atmosphere. We were usually able to convince them that it was in their best interests to go with Lucius, where they would be welcomed with open arms into the spirit world. Through force of circumstances we weren't able to continue with the group but I think it was very useful for the time we did it.

I asked Margaret Anna whether she had any further suggestions about how a group could function most effectively.

She replied, *'I have already mentioned open-mindedness, non-judgementalism and motivation. They are essential ingredients. It's also a big help if the individual members don't take themselves too seriously and feel that the burdens of the world are on their shoulders – or that their mission is to save all suffering souls. Ideally, we are all harbingers of joy – and, of course, helping to bring joy to troubled souls is the group's purpose. There's no need to get into any sort of ritualistic programme; in fact, that's undesirable because it would tend to impose a rigidity on the group.*

'Once they're open-minded and relaxed, the group members will find that inspiration will come to each of them as they go along. They needn't worry about whether they get any obvious physical evidence. They probably will, but if they don't it doesn't matter; as long as they trust in the process it will be effective.'

It's human nature to look for confirmation that a message has been received. Imagine you are concerned about someone and send them your love but don't get anything back. You don't know if it has worked. But Margaret Anna says that it is not necessary to await confirmation in this case.

'I don't want to suggest any rules of procedure. Each group will have its own way of working. As I keep saying, the way of spirit is spontaneous.'

Earthbound or trapped?

The discussions I had with Margaret Anna about the souls who found it difficult to leave the physical world were enlightening. However, because of the process by which we communicate – using thoughts rather than actual words – I wanted to confirm that I was using the correct terminology for the souls in question.

So I said to Margaret Anna, 'This is probably only a question of semantics, but I'm using the word "earthbound" to interpret what I feel you're conveying to me – as distinct from the word "trapped", which is often used for this connection. Which do you think is the more appropriate description, or is there any difference?'

Margaret Anna replied, *'I think the word "earthbound" is more accurate. The word "trapped" carries an implication that some outside agency is at work. It's of the utmost importance to remember that the type of isolation we're discussing is self-imposed. The word "earthbound" conveys exactly the factual situation, which is that souls who have left their physical bodies ("died", if you like, for the sake of clarity) continue, for one reason or another, to confine themselves to remaining within the earth's atmosphere.*

'I also feel that the word "earthbound" is more gentle than "trapped", which, I think, conveys an impression of torture. Many earthbound souls are quite happy to be in that situation and to remain so indefinitely. Of course there are also many

who are utterly miserable; these are the ones on whom we primarily focus our energies. At the same time, we don't neglect the others. If they show any signs of wanting to move on, we jump in immediately, so to speak, to offer our help.'

'But,' I asked, 'suppose I'm aware of a soul who is "living" in my house, and refuses to move on. What's the best course of action for me to follow?'

Margaret Anna replied, *'In a situation like that, a concern would be that the soul is drawing on your energy – and that of any other occupants of the house – so that it can remain attached to the heavy atmosphere of earth. On the assumption that you've tried, and are still trying, your best to help the soul to move on – and that you and any other occupants of the house have asked your guides to keep your auras clear of all negative energies, including all debilitating external energies – I can only suggest that you be patient. Remember, though, that you're not alone. Your guides and the earthbound soul's guides are continually trying to resolve the matter. Please always bear in mind that there's nothing to fear in situations like this.'*

When Margaret Anna mentioned the possibility that an earthbound soul might draw on my energy, she meant that because the soul no longer had the physical body it did when it was 'alive', it could be helped by staying close to me or other humans. In some ways, this is similar to someone miserable being energised by the presence of someone who is joyful.

It's understandable, but sad, that souls don't realise that they're 'dead'. Perhaps they simply don't want to leave familiar surroundings. However, it's equally comforting to know that there's so much help available from both spirit and human sources. Ultimately, any soul can be guided to spirit, where the welcome and the prospects of life in spirit will banish any earthly longings.

Chapter 11

The Commonality of Grief

One of the things that formed part of the religious teachings of my youth was the fact that, when people died, they lost contact with their relatives and friends on earth. They waited around to be judged (at least, as I imagined it) in a sort of comatose state until the Last Day, when the sheep will be separated from the goats, as it were. I don't know why the poor goats were selected as the symbolic representatives of those souls unfortunate enough to be consigned to eternal punishment.

I was musing on all that because Margaret Anna had mentioned that she would like to discuss further how souls in spirit continue to interact with people on earth.

She said, *'As we've seen, there are different levels of contact. Guides, for example, have agreements with those whom they guide, and are always instantly available to them. The contact is more sporadic where other souls are concerned.'*

She went on to tell me a story about continuing contact, concerning a woman called Jane who is another of Margaret Anna's 'charges'.

Jane is a woman in her 30s, happily married, with three children, aged six, four and two. The household revolves around her, and she looks after all the details of the domestic scene with superb efficiency.

She had launched a promising career as an interior designer, but she has put it on hold until the children are older. Her husband, Oliver, is a partner in a busy firm of accountants. Life is moving along smoothly and harmoniously for the family.

Jane has never suffered from anything other than minor illnesses, such as colds. When she begins to experience a nagging pain in her stomach, she ignores it for some time. She doesn't even mention it to Oliver. But it's not going away, so she decides to go to the family doctor. Because Jane trivialises the pain, the doctor doesn't take it too seriously and gives her a prescription for painkillers. He suggests that she return for a further consultation if the pain continues.

Jane experiences only minimal relief from the tablets. She goes back to the doctor, who arranges for her to go to hospital for tests. At this stage she feels she has to tell Oliver. Not surprisingly, Oliver is worried, but he convinces himself that because Jane has always seemed indestructible, the tests won't show anything serious.

Oliver's optimism proves to be unfounded. Jane is riddled with cancer. The medical prognosis is that she has, at the most, three months to live. And so it proves. The grief of the family knows no bounds as Jane's body gives up the struggle, and they're left helplessly wondering how they're going to manage without her.

Jane herself is devastated. She had tried to hold on, but even her powerful will had no chance against the cancer. When she leaves her body, she's in a state of utter distress at being separated from her family. She also carries the burden of their overwhelming sadness. She's around them all the time, but they're so numbed by their grief that they're not aware of her. She sees Oliver doing his best to organise things so that life can go on for the family in some fashion.

Margaret Anna knows that there's no point in trying to reach Jane while she's so enmeshed in her own grief and that of her family. In our time, there's an interval of nearly a year before Jane is ready to come to terms, even to a minor extent, with her new state. She has begun to relax a little as she sees that Oliver and the children have found a way of coping. She's had many bouts of exasperation because she's not there to sort things out when they get into a muddle, as they often do. No matter how hard she tries, she can't get through to any of them. However, they manage, somehow, to get by.

Margaret Anna has enlisted the help of Jane's father, Daniel, who died when Jane was only 15. They had loved each other very much. As Jane begins to relax, she becomes aware of her father. She's overjoyed to see him and they have a loving reunion. He talks to her and persuades her to go with him, constantly reassuring her that she'll continue to be able to be around her family.

They have arrived at a minor breakthrough. With the help of Daniel and other souls, Margaret Anna is able to show Jane that she can mind her family much more effectively by letting them go a little. The guides illustrate to her that her unbroken connection with her family is confusing them, because it sets up a vibration around them that they don't understand. It's a heavy vibration caused by her distress at her separation from them, and her inability to be physically there to take care of both them and all the details involved in managing the household. The guides arrange for her to meet other parents who have had to leave their families in somewhat similar situations. They invite her to join them in a cooperative grouping, whose aim is to be able to help the families they have left on earth, while finding ways to make progress on their own evolution. Soon she realises that she has immediate access to experts in all sorts of fields.

We here on earth are usually full of grief when our loved ones pass on. But we often, maybe usually, don't realise that the distress levels for the departed may be even greater than our own. In this case it was dreadful for Jane to be around her family and not to be able to connect with them or they with her.

In some cases the newly arrived soul in spirit connects immediately with family members who are already in spirit. It all depends on the states of mind people are in when they pass on. For instance if they don't believe they're dead or if, as in

Jane's case, they can't bear to tear themselves away from their loved ones, then it will take longer.

Margaret Anna said that Jane's case was quite common. If she could only have seen that she wasn't helping her family at all by staying around them in her state of distress and exasperation, things would have been so much easier for both them and herself. She would still have had all the sadness of separation (as would they); however, she would have been helped to realise very quickly that detaching from them to some extent didn't mean that she was abandoning them. The others in the group showed her very convincingly how well the liaising arrangements with their families' guides worked in practice.

I found it very interesting and helpful to hear how guides interact with souls who are in similar situations to Jane's and I wanted to know how usual that was.

Margaret Anna replied that it was becoming more so. She thinks it's an ideal arrangement. For example, Jane is introduced to the broad evolutionary picture involving herself and her family. She sees the purpose of the human tragedy in the context of what each family member set out to achieve through their lives on earth. Jane realises that she can meet them regularly while their bodies are asleep, and talk to them and listen to them and hold them close. Her children and her husband don't usually remember when they wake up – or, if they do, they'll probably convince themselves that they were dreaming. Still, they're likely to find that things that were bothering them before they went to sleep seem to have sorted themselves out – if only because they have a different way of looking at them – and they feel much better.

Jane sometimes wishes that they would be more aware of her. At the same time, she understands that it's best that they get on with their lives. She also knows that, in due course, she'll be able to meet them again in a more conscious way for all of them. In the meantime, because she's looking down from her 'helicopter', as it were, and has a panoramic view, she's able to mind them in ways that wouldn't have been open to her on earth. And by getting on with her own life and releasing herself to the joy of her changed state, she's spreading a loving vibration around her that includes her family in its embrace.

The power of dreams

In her story, Margaret Anna explained that Jane meets the members of her family regularly when they are asleep. Are we more conducive to visits from spirits when we are sleeping, I wondered?

I remember once listening to a radio programme, during which a psychologist was talking about dreams and their interpretation. A listener telephoned and said that his young daughter had died recently. Shortly after her death he had a vivid dream in which he met her. They had a wonderfully happy reunion and when he woke up he felt as if a huge weight of sadness had been lifted from him. He felt that he had really been with his daughter, but could he trust that feeling? The dream analyst's interpretation was to the effect that the man's subconscious had created the dream to help him deal with his grief, and that his daughter in the dream represented a healing aspect of himself. I had no doubt that the analyst's interpretation was not simply totally mistaken, but it very likely destroyed what had been for the distraught father a beautifully joyful, *real* experience. In my view he had experienced a meeting between himself and his daughter on the astral plane, a common description of where we go while our bodies are asleep (there's more about this in Chapter 12).

Throughout the ages, dreams have always provided a source of guidance for people. In my own case, one dream stands out vividly. I dreamt I was standing beside a gate, which Buddha was holding open. There were thousands and thousands of people coming towards the gate, but only small numbers going through it. Even though Buddha was looking at everybody with great love – and was obviously inviting them all to go through the gate, if they wished to do so – most of the people were ignoring him. They passed by the gate as if he wasn't there. After observing all that for a while, I asked Buddha how could he continue to project so much love towards everybody when he was being rejected by so many. He said to me, 'That's the way I am. The only way I can be.' He indicated that he was going to continue to hold the gate open until everybody came through it.

At the time I had that dream, I was newly into individual consultations. I thought that I'd be letting my guides down if I couldn't come up with a solution for every problem, no matter how intractable it seemed to be. I felt a huge sense of failure if no immediate solution emerged during the session, and I sometimes endured sleepless nights afterwards. The dream was as timely as it was helpful. Apart from the all-embracing love flowing from Buddha, which was relevant to every aspect of what I was doing, it showed me that the very best I could ever do would be to present myself as I was – with whatever I received from my guides – and then to allow the outcome to be whatever it would be.

Incidentally, while I had known about Buddha, I hadn't previously had any particular interest in him or Buddhism, nor have I developed any since. I have, however, always felt deeply grateful for that experience.

Letting go

It is not just souls who find it difficult to let go of their physical existence on earth, lost in feelings of bereavement. Humans, too, can continue to grieve for a lost child, lover, parent or friend, and find it difficult to let go.

Margaret Anna commented, *'Partings are an inevitable consequence of the temporary nature of the human condition, with death being seen as the final one. As we know, it's not (or what am I at?). There are always good reasons for them in overall evolutionary patterns.*

'What can I say? It's a matter of profound regret that the experience of humanness is still so painful for so many souls. We can't interfere with free will. All we can do is try to lighten the burden of suffering to the best of our abilities. The more people accept that there's no final parting, and that continuing contact between the physical and spirit states is possible, the more we hope and expect that the grief of separation will be lessened.'

As I see it, grief is an inbuilt feature of life on earth. It's an ironic fact that from the moment we're born, we're dying. Even as we grow into the fullness of our youthful vigour and physical prowess, we're constantly reminded of death – in our immediate families and our friends and acquaintances – and through news reports, death notices in newspapers, wars and natural disasters. As day passes day, we're that little bit nearer to the inevitable end of our physical existence.

That's a morbid way of looking at life and it's best that we don't indulge ourselves in it. If we can see it as a temporary experiment in helping us to become ever closer to a level of consciousness that's in complete alignment with unconditional love, we can enjoy the experiment, even while as human beings we're not exempt from experiencing deep levels of grief throughout our lives. The grief will be more bearable for us when we can see it in the wider context of continuing life, as Margaret Anna suggests.

Some years ago a man named Louis, who happened to be a doctor involved in cancer research, came to see me. His wife, Pamela, to whom he had been very close, had recently died, leaving him with a young family of three children, all of whom were girls. He was disconsolate, not just because of the loss of his beloved partner, but because he couldn't take away the burden of grief from his children. He also felt helpless because Pamela had managed all of the household affairs; he didn't know how he was going to be able to cope with them all – as well as with the needs (in particular, emotional needs) of young girls growing up.

It turned out to be a most unusual case for me. I agreed to meet him on a fairly regular basis (which wasn't my usual practice), because initially I felt very sorry for him and, as time went on, we became good friends. What was really wonderful about his case for both of us was that Pamela always came through as clearly as if she were sitting with us (which she was, of course, now that I think of it). She had answers for all of his questions, as well as most helpful advice about the children. It's important to say that she didn't intrude into any areas that the children might have wanted to keep secret from him, which meant that he had no qualms about passing on to them detailed information about what transpired at our meetings. The result was that the whole family felt that Pamela was looking after them in a totally loving way. She, in turn, had the consolation of knowing that they were aware of that, and was comforted by the fact that she was able to anticipate things for them from a broader canvas than would have been possible on earth. An added bonus was that she was able to provide insights for him into challenges that kept cropping up for him in his work, particularly to do with his research.

Sadly, from a physical point of view, he was another of my friends who left his body some years ago. I'm sure there was a joyful reunion with Pamela, and that both of them have continued to help their children (who are now adults). I also hope that, by now, more than likely, he has had fruitful findings in his research towards lessening suffering on earth.

In most cases the contact isn't so obvious as it was in that one, in which I felt privileged to have been a link. One of my reasons for telling the story is that I believe that the contact is always there, and the people concerned can become more aware of it as they open themselves to its possibility and – I'm convinced – its certainty.

Grief has many guises

Of course, physical death is not the only – or even the most devastating – cause of grief. I have met many people who were grieving over a multiplicity of things, such as problems within families, broken relationships (particularly where long-standing friendships were involved), unhappiness in work situations, and unrequited love. Sometimes it became possible for people to see that what they felt were sources of grief could be transformed into valid reasons for rejoicing.

There was, however, one case where I had to admit to utter failure. A young woman called Sally was totally infatuated – she called it in love – with a well-known pop star. She had never met him. Sally was convinced that he shared her passionate love, although she didn't have any evidence to support her conviction. What she wanted me to tell her was that they were going to live happily ever after in blissful togetherness. No matter how much I tried to shift her on to other aspects of her life, I couldn't divert her from her obsession and, of course, I couldn't tell her what she wanted to hear. After about three hours, in a state of complete exhaustion, I managed to bring the meeting to an end.

My reason for mentioning this case is that, in my experience, obsessions (often of a totally irrational kind) are a major cause of grief. I think all humans suffer from them to some degree. The possibilities for developing obsessions are wide-ranging; for example, sport, sex, drugs, religious fanaticism, controlling tendencies, gambling, alcohol, judgementalism, possessiveness, making money, careers, perceptions of success or failure, and so on and on.

I suggest that it might be an interesting exercise for people to consider to what extent, if any, they suffer from obsessiveness. Any form of it is a barrier to freedom of thought. As human beings, it's unlikely that we'll be able to free ourselves from all forms of it but, if we can become aware of an area or areas where we're inclined to immerse ourselves in it, that awareness can help us to regard it as part of our human foibles. In that way it can help us to experience freedom in our thought processes.

No matter where we go in our exploration of life in the physical and non-physical dimensions, we're inevitably brought back to the need for open-mindedness.

The role of religion

In resuming discussion with Margaret Anna, I couldn't resist commenting that, when we look at the whole area of death and the grief that accrues from it, I think it's fair to say that religions – at least Christian religions – haven't been very helpful. As far as I know, they would still be dismissive of the possibility – not to mention the desirability – of the sort of continuing contact that we were discussing. Indeed, any idea of the validity of Margaret Anna communicating with me would surely be seen as a projection of my crazed imagination.

Margaret Anna said, *'Still, religions do provide comfort for many people. And, of course, it's central to religious teaching that life continues after death. Even the notion of eternal damnation in Hell can be put into the context of tormented states of mind, as we saw in the case of Alfredo; in such a state, a moment is an eternity.*

'Fear and obedience to authority were very much the base of religious tradition, as perceived by many of its adherents. But that's changing.

Except where extreme fundamentalism is concerned, a positive approach tends to be emphasised rather than a negative one; in other words, compassion, tolerance and love, rather than fear.

'All the same, I'd say that you'd be on to a good thing if you were to bet against our communications being received with open arms – not to mention open minds – by religious orthodoxy. What's new?'

There's always hope.

Chapter 12

Exploring Our Communication with Guides

Now that Margaret Anna has provided extensive illustration of what life is like in spirit, I feel that it's a timely opportunity for me to explore further the whole area of communication with guides. Much of this has been conveyed to me by my spirit guides, and through my own experience over many years of working with them in my own life, in individual consultations with people and in running workshops. I cannot, however, fully discuss the role that guides play in our lives without considering where 'free will' fits into the equation.

By the way, in what I'm writing I hope I don't sound dogmatic. It would be tedious if I had to preface everything with statements such as 'my understanding is', or words to that effect, so I'm going to use a direct style. You will realise by now that when I make statements about life in spirit they come from information I have been given by my guides.

All souls have free will, and can choose whether they wish to incarnate or reincarnate in physical bodies. As we are all part of

God/unconditional love, there can be no conditions attached to how we use our free will. (There are, of course, ultimately self-imposed consequences, as Margaret Anna has illustrated in the stories about Johann and Alfredo.) It's open to us to choose whether we want guides to help us during our lives on earth. Those guides are evolved souls who are familiar with conditions on earth and who have already learned the lessons it has to offer.

As I thought about it, it seemed perfectly natural and logical that it should be so. In the physical world the vast majority of people are willing to help each other when they're aware of a need to do so. I know that's not the impression we may get from reading newspapers, or listening to radio or television news items. Stories about man's inhumanity to man are, perhaps understandably, perceived to be more newsworthy than those depicting tolerance and love. It's the former that come to our attention most frequently – and persistently. That has its own merits, in that cruelties, etc., are highlighted; however, it presents an unbalanced view, in a negatively slanted way, of how things are.

Certainly, in my now lengthy experience, I have rarely met an unkind or unhelpful person. As an aside, I considered making an exception of a teacher in a primary school that I had to attend for a couple of years when I was about six or seven years old. She used the leg of a chair to inflict punishment. Even when I knew the answers I was unable to verbalise them; apart from my nervousness, I knew from experience that being right was no guarantee of escaping her wrath. A sure sign of what was to come was when her false teeth began to clack and the top teeth dropped onto the bottom ones. However, in the mellowness of my advanced years, I can say that outside of school she was regarded as a hearty, friendly person, and she probably saw herself as having the best interests of her pupils at heart. So I won't make an exception of her, tempting as it is!

Things have changed considerably, even in the space of my lifetime. For example, the approach to teaching personified by the chair-woman would now be inconceivable. As people grow in awareness they automatically want to make the world a better and happier place for everybody. If that happens within the restrictive framework of the physical world, it surely stands to reason that as souls move into higher vibrations they are even more inclined to help those of us who are still struggling with the human dimension.

Getting to know the guides

When I began to ask my guides for help, at the outset of my communication with them, I was concerned that I'd be letting myself in for a lot of pain and suffering. I had no doubt that they would always operate in my best spiritual interests, but my childhood and adolescent experiences had cemented in me the belief that there could be no spiritual growth without suffering. With the 'way of the cross' weighing heavily on my mind, it took me quite some time before I could accept that planet earth was never intended to be a vale of tears – and that life on it could, ideally, and in accordance with my higher spiritual purpose, be experienced as a joyful adventure rather than a painful one. Asking my guides for help brought with it an assurance that I would be nudged along paths that would be rosy rather than thorny or that, even if the thorns couldn't be completely removed, their sharpness would be dulled.

In the early stages of my adult consciousness of guides, such as Margaret Anna, I wanted to know all about them. That was also true of people I met. We're so used to placing everything in boxes and labelling them that it was understandable that we'd want to do the same with our guides. I expected to have the type of communication we have here on earth, with questions fully answered in a straightforward manner, when I asked them. I expected to learn intimate details about my guides that would fit in with my own experience of people.

The reality could not have been more different. Sometimes I'd get some information – such as a name or names – but more usually what I got was doled out in a meagre sort of way. Eventually I came to realise that our guides were – and are – seeking to help us grow out of confined, literal, black-and-white patterns of thinking. When I obsessively tried to personalise my guides, I wanted to bring them down to my level in a literal way. They were, however, seeking to help me to raise myself to their level and, in the process, to see myself in a much more expansive way than I had been used to. The ironic thing was that, once I understood that, the labels weren't important and so became more readily available.

During one of his meditations, a man named Donald was given the name 'Beelezebub' as that of one of his guides. To say that he was taken aback would be a major understatement! His understanding of the name was that it belonged to the Prince of Devils — Satan himself, the ultimate personification of evil. Did that mean that he himself was irretrievably caught in the grip of darkness? Yet the only feeling coming to him from the guide was one of great love. When he accepted that Beelezebub was only a name — in fact, a rather nice-sounding one — and that he was being guided *not* to take up positions on the basis of his conditioning and absolutist tendencies, he had no difficulty. He even learned to play with the name, when he wanted to — and call the guide 'Beeleze' or 'Bub'. Guides don't mind what they're called.

That story brings up a commonly asked question. How can we be sure that it is our guide or guides communicating with us, and not some less-evolved or mischievous spirit? Shebaka had a good answer to that question.

He said, *'If you make a conscious decision to ask your guides for help, they will see to it that no other spirit can communicate with you without invitation on your part. Remember that you make the decision. If you don't ask for their help, the guides cannot impose themselves on you.*

That's the nature of love; it never seeks to possess or impose. There's no limit to the amount of help available to you; if there is a limit, it will have been set by you.'

In that context, I think it's good to remind ourselves that when it comes to material problems, such as difficulties with plumbing, electrical gadgets, cars, computers and so on, we have no hesitation about asking for help from those whom we regard as experts in their particular fields. It's surely obvious that the same thing applies in asking for help from the experts in spirit. I doubt if few of us could say that we don't need it.

Working with groups

When I did individual 'readings' I needed to get direct information and to trust that whatever I received was in the best interests of the people concerned. Apart from one case, which I described earlier (about the imminent death of a woman's mother) I don't remember ever getting information that I would be hesitant about passing on. I stopped doing individual sessions after about eighteeen years, as I wanted to devote more time to working with groups and to writing. Apart from the fact that I no longer had the energy to cope with the insatiable demand for individual consultations, I believed that in the long run it would be far more helpful for people to find ways of getting their own answers rather than coming to someone like me for them.

In the group situations we attempted to find the style of communication that suited each person. For example, we considered how impressions normally came to each individual in the group. Questions like these were relevant: Do you tend to get visual images easily? Do you operate more on a feeling level? Are you comfortable with ideas? Do you understand things better when you write them down? Do you find that you just know things at times without having to go through a logical process to work them out? The answers to questions such as those showed how the participants' guides would tend to develop communication with them through their particular styles.

I mentioned earlier that the three most important elements involved in achieving direct communication with guides were relaxation, patience and trust. Of the three, I regarded relaxation as being the most difficult. Any form of anxiety, for example 'trying too hard', creates a blockage.

Suppose you have a problem, or a decision to make. You decide that you're going to ask your guides a direct question about it. You sit as comfortably as you can. You have arranged to have no interruptions, and then you ask your question. You find, though, that random thoughts keep intruding. What about this, that or the other? Did I forget to do something that I should have done? What time is it? Should I have collected my son from school? What should I have for dinner? The list goes on.

How do you stop that from happening? It's very difficult to control our thoughts by consciously trying to do so. Instead of trying to brush them aside, try observing each thought as it impinges on your consciousness. Hold it steady, without reacting to it in any way – even if the thought itself is disagreeable. After a little while it will fade away. Repeat the process for other thoughts as you become aware of them. Soon you will find that the thoughts are no longer crowding in on you, and that your mind will grow still. Then you're in a better position to ask your question.

A colleague in my first work assignment had a stock phrase that he occasionally trotted out: 'Resist not evil, says St Paul.' It stayed in my mind because it struck me as incongruous that St Paul could have said something that seemed to be incompatible with Christian teaching. (I seem to remember I found, when I looked it up, that the statement was attributed to Jesus, rather than Paul.) With the passage of time, and in my more awakened state, I realised that what was meant was that resistance always reinforces; by fighting against something – such as an emotion like fear – we feed it and strengthen it. When we take up fixed positions on right and wrong, good or bad, we get lost in a tangle of wasted energy and our minds can't reach the stillness they crave.

So the relaxation bit works, your mind is still and you've asked your question. Now be patient and see what answer comes to you. It will probably appear in a form that best suits your style. Trust it, if you can, and see what happens.

In my workshops we usually found that looking at the participants' auras individually was interesting and informative. I simply asked one participant at a time to sit against a white or brightly coloured wall; the rest of us looked in as relaxed a way as we could at his or her forehead and then let our eyes drift around the body.

Nearly everybody in my groups was successful at seeing auras – if not immediately, then at some point during each course. Most were able to see colours; others could only see white light around the person under scrutiny. It was exciting when people saw shapes of light moving around the person. Usually, spirit guides show themselves in that way. We did lots of experiments in communication; for example, we accessed past lives and got information that was usually very relevant to the present lives of the people concerned. Most of the participants gained confidence in their own styles of communication. We had great fun, too!

Given that guides cannot be present physically, communication has to be arranged rather like a telephone conversation – but minus the sound. When somebody contacts you by telephone, you're aware of the caller before you can hear a voice and you don't have to pinch yourself and ask: 'Is it my imagination playing tricks on me?' Before you lift the telephone you get a signal – the ringing tone – and you know that there's somebody at the other end of the line. Similarly, you can arrange to have a signalling system with a guide or guides that will be your way of satisfying yourself that you are having authentic communication. If you want to have a chat with a guide, you could ask the guide for a signal that you can continue to use as a lead in to your communication. The signal could be a visual image, a shivery or a tingly feeling, a word, an impression of being touched, or perhaps a feeling of an in-flow of energy or being gently rocked. The main thing is that it should be an easy signal that would also be unmistakable.

Nudges from our guides

A question that has been frequently asked during discussions in which I have been involved is how to distinguish between 'imagination' and communication from guides. I have to admit that this is a question with which I have struggled myself. I find that the more relaxed and non-judgemental I am – without allowing wishful thinking to influence me – the less I'm prey to doubts about whether my guides are getting through to me or not.

I always like to get signs or 'auguries' that the lines of communication with my guides are working. Sometimes I ask for them just for the fun of it; at other times they come unex-pectedly. The following is an example.

Some years ago I needed to rearrange an appointment with a man named Mike. I called the number I had for him, and when a male voice answered I asked if he was Mike.

The voice said, 'Yes.'

When I began to explain what I wanted, he interrupted me to say that he wasn't the man I was looking for. Remarkably, though, his name was also Mike. Strangely, too, this 'Mike' had been thinking of ringing me. He didn't know the other Mike and, of course, his telephone number was different. How I got through to him was a mystery.

Following our conversation, he participated in a course I was running, one morning a week over a period of eleven weeks. On the last morning of the course he told us that he had been notified the previous week that he would be needed as a witness in a court case that was due to be held on the morning of our meeting. He said to his guides that they would have to make sure that he wouldn't miss the last part of the course. He informed the legal people that he had a prior engagement that he couldn't cancel, and that they could contact him on his mobile telephone when he was due to be called to the witness stand. Shortly before we finished he got a call to say that the case had been settled and he wasn't needed.

I don't know what combination of circumstances led to the settlement but, presumably, it was the best solution for both parties. In any event, Mike's guides came up trumps not only for Mike – but also for the rest of us in the group, who bene-fited very much from his presence.

In the following story, I hadn't asked for a sign but it came anyway.

Before I got round to being able, after a fashion, to use a computer, I had a very accommodating typewriter that allowed me to type laboriously on it with one finger. The day after I had typed some comments about guardian angels, I went out to have photocopies made. On my way back I remembered that I wanted to buy something. I was drawn to go into a particular shop. A pleasant, serious-looking woman took my order. As she was handing me the item, her whole countenance lit up with a beautiful smile and she said: 'There you are, angel.'

Perhaps having noticed my somewhat mystified expression as I thanked and paid her, she explained: 'I heard you speak.'

That was all. She went back to what she had been doing before serving me, and I left the shop. I think I was too awed – not so much by the incident itself (although the woman had given me a lovely gift for which I was very grateful) but by its timing – to ask her for elaboration.

On the face of it, that was only a minor, passing happening; but, to me, it was a wonderful affirmation of how angels reveal themselves to us and encourage us, if we're open-minded enough to allow them to do so.

Once again, however, revelations don't always come directly; for example, they often happen through other people, through hearing a song or a piece of music, or reading something. Our guides are infinitely ingenious in finding ways to communicate with us, even if we are totally unconscious of them. When they communicate, the primary consideration for guides is to help people raise their levels of awareness, so it's always important to remember that answers may not come in a literal way. This story may help to illustrate that point.

A woman named Antoinette telephoned me on a Friday evening to say that she was due to be married in two weeks. The invitations had gone out and all arrangements had been made. However, her fiancé had just told her that he couldn't go ahead with the marriage. She was devastated. She was due to go away for the weekend with friends, but she couldn't face that now. She asked me if I could consult my guides and ask them to talk to her fiancé's guides, in order to change his mind.

I couldn't agree to ask that of my guides – which would be an interference with free will – but she wasn't in any mood for philosophical arguments. I asked for guidance and I told her that the message I was getting was that the whole situation would be sorted out by the following Monday.

She called me again on Monday evening. After talking with me on Friday, she had assumed that her fiancé would contact her on Monday to say that he had suffered a temporary aberration and now couldn't wait to be married to her. She was delighted by the prospect, and happily went off on her weekend, which she thoroughly enjoyed. But when she got back her fiancé informed her that, far from changing his mind, he was even more firmly entrenched in his decision not to marry her. So, she wanted to know, what was I, or my guides, or both, up to in assuring her that the situation would be sorted out by Monday?

Although by that stage of my own journey I had come to realise that, as a general rule, guidance isn't meant to be taken too literally, I was taken aback and, indeed, beginning to feel responsible for having created the whole situation. All I could do was talk to her and listen. As we talked, it began to emerge that what was really troubling her was that all the invitations had gone out, presents had been received, and the prospect of cancelling a wedding was hugely embarrassing. When it came down to the nitty-gritty of it, she, in her heart, wasn't happy about marrying him either. With this knowledge, her mood changed completely. She said she'd contact him straight away and tell him that she agreed with his decision. She would wish him well in his life, and then she'd deal with the situation about the invitations and the gifts.

She subsequently contacted me to confirm that she had done all that and had then gone off on a lovely holiday. Not long afterwards she met another man; they got married and were very happy. Years later I was privileged to meet her husband.

I remember her and the incident with much gratitude. She helped me to develop more trust in the wonder of the grand design of life. She had badly needed to have a joyful weekend. Something had shifted for her over the weekend and, even though she felt completely let down on the following Monday, she was more receptive to looking at the whole situation in a different way. Once we got to the core of what was really troubling her, everything changed.

As I have so often been told, there's no limit to the help available. All we have to do is ask – but it's important not to try and put hooks on the outcome.

An element of surprise

I now employ a handing-over process in my day-to-day life, rather than looking for answers. I put my trust in my guides, and know that my concerns and worries will be resolved in an appropriate fashion. This approach leaves me more open to the wonder of how things happen, without confining them by any of my own expectations. Margaret Anna once remarked that a nice thing about being human is that one can enjoy surprises – if they're nice ones!

The astral plane

When a soul in spirit decides that its evolution will be enhanced by incarnating or reincarnating, it leaves the freedom of the spirit dimension for the restrictiveness of the physical one. It's easy enough to imagine what a huge shock this must be. In order to ease the shock, the body is designed with an in-built need for sleep. While the body is asleep, the soul is free from the limitation of its temporary physical cage and can travel to what is known as the 'astral plane'. It is much like travelling through the sky, while staying in fairly close proximity to the sleeping body. The astral plane can't be described as a place as such, because it's not defined by physical boundaries. The soul can then do the sort of things that Margaret Anna outlined in her story of Jane, who continued her contact with her children while they were asleep.

Our guides can arrange to sort things out while we're asleep. For example, suppose I have a forthcoming meeting that I'm hoping will turn out well for me. Before I go to sleep the night before the meeting, I can ask my guides to arrange to set up the meeting on the astral plane, so that there is a positive atmosphere around it. When I actually go to the meeting in my awakened state, the energy and the outcome will be as positive as I would wish them to be. I can do the same thing in any situation that concerns me. I often suggest this approach to others, while reminding them that guides can't interfere with a soul's free will.

I mentioned earlier that, when he was on earth, my friend Frank was involved in helping people. He has continued to do so by easing the transition of souls from the physical to the spirit state. In doing my individual 'readings', I often found that people's 'dead' relatives or friends had a cooperative arrangement with the guides of the people in question to help them. This arrangement has a two-way benefit in that it helps both parties – physical and spirit. For example, while she was on earth it might have been a totally alien concept for someone's grandmother to think she could continue contact with a beloved grandchild after her passing. However, as she becomes more familiar with life in spirit she becomes aware that such contact is possible, and that she can liaise with her grandchild's guides in order to help him or her. In this way she's also helped in her own evolution towards increased awareness and her grandchild may find the familiarity of the contact with his or her grandmother an easy and natural arrangement.

Going solo

At one stage I asked Margaret Anna a rather frivolous question.

'Suppose,' I said, 'I don't want to bother with guides. If I'd rather work things out under my own steam, do you have any helpful suggestions?'

Margaret Anna replied, *'Is there an implication that I might make unhelpful suggestions? Of course, that would be your own choice. I assume your question is hypothetical, unless it's an indirect way of sacking me!*

'Our role as guides is to help souls to connect more fully with their own divinity. Meditation can be helpful in that context – it is anyway, whether you're using your guides or not. As long as your intention is to allow yourself to flow more and more with your divine energy, it doesn't much matter what form of meditation you use – nor do you need to set up any ritual around it. Do, if you like, of course.

'I must do the public-relations bit, though! Suppose you're due to travel to a location that is, say, fifty miles (or its equivalent) from your present one. You have only two choices – either you take a bus or a train or you walk. Which would you choose? You'll get there either way, but the journey will certainly take much longer if you walk. Your feet, and probably other parts of you, are likely to be sore. Guides, like the bus or the train, would help to take the weight off your feet, in a manner of speaking.'

As it happened, when I was writing down her answer I was in an aeroplane flying to San Diego. I asked her why we usually refer to the world of spirit as being 'up there'. 'Up here in midair, am I closer to that world? If the plane crashes I certainly will be!'

She replied, 'It's logical enough. To be as light as air is a common expression. In spirit we're in a lighter vibration than that of earth. We are not controlled by gravity like you are. Showing wings on angels is a symbolic way of illustrating the freedom and lightness of spirit.'

All of us can ask for help directly when we feel we need it, by sending out our request then being still and waiting for the answer. That answer will come, whether we use our guides 'up there' or not. It may not come in the way we expected or hoped, but it will come in a way that benefits us most in the evolutionary scale of things.

Chapter 13

Free Will in Practice

Consideration of the notion of free will seems to introduce an element of ambiguity. Do we have free will, or don't we? If we do, is it total or limited?

As I mentioned earlier, a question that's often asked is: if there really is a God/Supreme Being, why does He allow such awful atrocities to happen in the world? If He's all-powerful, as He's represented to be, how can He permit so many of his 'children'(as human beings tend to be classified) to be brutally victimised and abused?

A common answer is that God has given us free will. Depending on how we use it, we will be rewarded or punished by Him, in Heaven or in Hell, for all eternity. Of course, if we accept that scenario, we're effectively accepting the idea that God must be an unimaginably cruel dictator. How could anyone who claims to 'love' us allow such things?

However, if we get rid of the idea of separateness and accept that we're all *part* of God (or unconditional love, which, I think, is an easier description), in order to move us out of our conditioned way of thinking, then the whole situation is relieved of its ambiguity. In that case it makes no sense to blame God for the atrocities. Responsibility for them lies with people who have separated themselves from their divine essence (like Alfredo, for instance), through their abuse of their free will.

Margaret Anna commented: *'Humans generally have been conditioned to an ambiguous view of free will. On the one hand, they're told that they have it; on the other hand, they're also told that it's subject to divine laws. But to be free is to be without conditions or limitations.*

'It's easy to see how confusion arises. Democratic societies subscribe to a philosophy that people are free to live their lives as they choose. Yet those same societies enact laws which, if broken, lead to punishment – often by imprisonment. So, then, there's free will in theory, but it's subject to conditions in practice.

'There are frequent proclamations to the effect that what's neatly called the rule of law must prevail so that people can live together peaceably. New laws are framed, and existing laws are amended, or annulled, according to politicians' perceptions of predominant public moods.'

I asked, 'But doesn't all that add up to the people saying that they choose to exercise their free will by having such laws enacted on their behalf?'

Margaret Anna replied, *'It would if you had 100 per cent agreement. Otherwise you have imposition of will by one group on another. However, may we leave all that argument aside for the present? What I'm trying to explain is how people automatically regard themselves as having free will only up to a point. It seems logical to assume that the same thing applies in spirit realms.*

'*You may remember that I talked earlier about the challenge of freedom. People expect to be regulated because they don't know anything else. Souls in spirit, on the other hand, are being guided towards coming to terms with existence in a dimension where there's no regulation.*

'*It just can't be that a soul doesn't have total freedom of choice about whether to incarnate or reincarnate, or the environment into which to be born. Anything else would be a restriction of its free will, its divine nature, which knows no limitation. In its exercise of free will it may, of course, seek guidance, which is readily available.*'

She suggested that perhaps she could shed more light on the question of choice by giving me an illustration of how it works in practice.

Back in the Middle Ages, somewhere in Europe, a boy whom Margaret Anna called Cyprian – not his real name – was born. He was an intelligent boy and was particularly agile in discussion and debate. It was no surprise when he gravitated to the Church and, in due course, became a bishop.

He liked power and he used it to his own advantage. He had no doubts about his intellectual capacity, and, in his view, he had no equal. He lived sumptuously and didn't deny himself in any aspect of life. There was no question of celibacy, as far as he was concerned. Women were there to be used and discarded at his pleasure, without any regard for their feelings. Because of his position and reputation nobody dared to say 'no' to him; those who had done so early on in his 'reign' were harshly punished – often fatally.

They were cruel times. People's free will didn't count for much. Inquisitional proceedings were widespread, with Cyprian as an ardent supporter. He wrote cleverly argued dissertations in favour of the most severe punishments for those who were accused of heretical practices or leanings – and they were many. It was an easy way to dispose of any unwanted relatives or potential rivals or nonconformists.

Cyprian's fame spread, bringing him favourable notice in papal circles, resulting in his promotion to Archbishop and, later, Cardinal. With the expansion of his area of influence came increased power, with correspondingly greater scope for satisfying indiscriminate voraciousness.

He ruled for many years with no lessening of his abusive power. The only thing that he couldn't control was his own mortality, and eventually he succumbed to it. Many lavish tributes were paid to him on his death, and he was acclaimed as a saint.

There was no miraculous transformation at his transition. He carried his arrogance with him, and changing awareness was a slow process for him. Eventually, however, he allowed himself to be helped and he came to some understanding of the extent of his abuse of power. There was no condemnation, other than from himself.

It was a difficult stage for him. He decided that he would have to make reparation to the victims of his abuse and he sought guidance as to how he could do so. Various options, including reincarnation, were presented to him. It was stressed that there was no obligation to choose any of the options – that, indeed, he didn't need to. Whatever choice he made, he would be helped to put it into operation.

The other options would have involved him remaining in spirit. These included seeking individual forgiveness from everyone whom he had abused when he had an opportunity to do so, and helping, in whatever way he could, souls who were finding it difficult to adjust to being in spirit.

The upshot of all his considerations was that he chose to be born as a female child in an impoverished African environment. The reason why he chose to be female was because of his sexual abuse of many women. He wanted to be able to experience in some way the pain that he had caused them. Remember that it's the soul's journey – the gender is incidental.

In the lifetime that ensued, Cyprian experienced the ravages of poverty, internecine warfare and multiple rapes. There were many times when he, as the young woman, wished for death, but it was slow in coming. Finally it did, as a result of one more brutal rape.

I think it's important to draw attention to the fact that the stories told by Margaret Anna are accounts of actual happenings, although the names have been changed – in the same way as the stories I have included were factual, although I have concealed the identity of the persons concerned unless they gave me permission to reveal it. Some of Margaret Anna's stories are necessarily stark because they record details of how free will was abused and the consequences that flowed from that abuse.

I felt I needed to get clarification from Margaret Anna about Cyprian's case. He had abused power in extreme ways, including rape. In order to compensate for that, he chose a lifetime where he knew he would be a victim of utter degradation and abuse. I asked her if it was fair to draw a general conclusion from Cyprian's story that, if I am an abuser (in whatever form) in one lifetime, I am likely to choose to be a victim in another.

Margaret Anna replied, *'There's no hard and fast rule; in fact, as I keep saying, there are no rules at all in spirit.'*

She explained that one of the choices available to Cyprian – in his perception of his situation – was to find ways to make reparation to each of his victims individually. But there were so many of them that, in Cyprian's opinion, it would have been a completely unrealistic option. He asked himself how he could ever forgive himself if he couldn't somehow share the suffering he had imposed on his victims. Ultimately, he chose what seemed to him the best way to do that. After his transition from the later life he was able to begin the process of forgiving himself.

Divine nature

The ultimate 'sin', in Margaret Anna's opinion, is betrayal of our divine natures – love. We have all 'sinned' in this way – all of us who have been through the earth experience and some who haven't. We can only restore ourselves fully to the expression of our divine natures when we forgive ourselves completely for our betrayal.

The notion of punishment has been so much a part of our human conditioning for so long that it's very hard to get rid of it. Margaret Anna said that it was fascinating to see the reaction of souls (after they had left their physical bodies and adjusted to the spirit state) when they realised that punishment didn't fit into the scheme of things in spirit. More often than not, there was a mixture of shock, incredulity, surprise and then exhilaration.

I asked what was, perhaps, an obvious question: 'In Cyprian's case, when he realised that no heavenly judge was going to punish him, couldn't he just have said, "Well, that's fine" – or words to that effect – and got on with his new life without bothering to make reparation?'

Margaret Anna replied, *'It was open to him to do so. However, he couldn't – I mean he found it impossible to do so. How can I explain? Imagine a huge room, which is brilliantly lit with hundreds of incandescent bulbs. One by one the bulbs are dimmed until the room is in darkness.*

'Let's say that the soul Cyprian is a room in all its shining brightness. As he betrayed his divine nature over and over again, he dimmed
the lights, bit by bit. He had taken away his capacity to see. Once he
realised what he had done, he wanted to be able to see as he had originally – which meant restoring the room to its former brightness.

'I used the rough analogy of the room because I wanted to show that
there was an easier way towards "redemption" than that chosen by
Cyprian. How could he restore the room to its former brightness?
Simply by pressing a switch. The switch is self-forgiveness for his lack
of awareness in his human state.'

I said, 'I can imagine all sorts of objections to that as being
far too easy. Wouldn't there be an outcry from all his victims at
him getting off scot-free like that? Are you saying that all somebody – who might have committed the most heinous crimes
against humanity – need do is forgive himself and that takes
care of everything for him?'

Margaret Anna replied, 'Before he could get round to forgiving
himself, he'd have to understand what he was forgiving himself for. The
extent of his blindness would be apparent to him before he could restore
his sight. He'd have reached a stage where he would be incapable of
committing any of those crimes again.'

I said, 'There's an old saying to the effect that to understand
all is to forgive all. Is that what you mean?'

Margaret Anna replied, 'Exactly. When a soul reaches a stage of
being open to seeing the film of its complete evolution to date, it can
observe all of its ups and downs, its acts of cruelty and compassion, its

expressions of hate and love – like a seesaw, always struggling for balance and never succeeding. When it had a life as an abuser, it was likely to have sought to balance it by being a victim in another life, on a scale equal to that of the abuse in so far as that could be estimated; in the long run, a never-ending cycle of repetition going nowhere.

'Everything in spirit is simple. We're trying to bring similar simplicity into human consciousness. When we – and by "we" I mean every soul who has ever taken on a physical body – examine the history of our evolution, we soon see that we could never make adequate reparation for our abuse of our divine natures, no matter how much we might choose to punish ourselves. When we come to an acceptance of that, and admit to ourselves that we expressed our free will idiotically – that we regret what we did, but that we can't turn the clock back – we reach a haven of understanding that, mercifully, we can release ourselves to the fullness of divine love in us by forgiving ourselves.'

Is free will a burden?

Would we be better off if we didn't have free will at all? That's a question that has often been asked during the discussions in which I have participated. For thousands of years we've been going round in circles, getting caught in the seesaw of cause and effect. Maybe it would be reasonable to expect that a benevolent deity might have made things easier for us by mapping out, step by step, the way we should live our lives. We wouldn't be held responsible for our actions because we wouldn't be faced with choices. We'd be like dogs on leads – dogs who are well looked after.

The version of Christianity into which I was inducted in my youth taught me that I had free will. But I was given a set of rules that I had to obey, or I would be punished forever by the Supreme Being that made the rules. So it was a type of 'conditional' free will.

Yet, in spite of all the twists and turns and traumas involved, I know I wouldn't like to have a restriction on my free will. I'm very glad that there cannot be any restriction on it, since that would be a negation of my divine nature. In other words, I wouldn't exist as I am – I'd be a sort of robot. That wouldn't appeal to me at all, no matter how many times I might have craved for some form of oblivion.

The trouble with having free will is that there's a huge onus on us to use it appropriately. It seems that there's no sphere of life where we don't seek to impose our will on each other, whether consciously or unconsciously. That's obvious in the big arenas, such as wars, but it can be extremely subtle and insidious in personal interaction. It's the simplest thing in the world for me to convince myself that I'm acting in the best interests of people, by manipulating them in directions that I think are best for them. I can feel good then when I'm arranging the world along the best possible lines – as I see them, of course!

Let's say that I'm the parent of a daughter who is in a relationship that I regard as unsuitable. I believe that it will lead to unhappiness for her. I feel that it's my duty to use my influence in whatever way I can to get her out of the relationship. In my view I'm acting in her best interests. That's just my opinion, of course. What I'm doing may persuade my daughter to take a direction in her life that's completely contrary to what she set out to achieve in it. In my ignorance I'm unwittingly harming instead of helping her.

As humans, we're being challenged to find freedom in the way we think. According to the French philosopher René Descartes, '*Cogito ergo sum*' – 'I think, therefore I am'. Does it follow that if I think free, I am therefore free? No, but in my opinion it follows that the only way I can be free is in my thoughts. I exercise my free will in how I put my thoughts into action. I can think what I like and people don't know what I'm thinking unless I choose to tell them. How I think affects how I am, of course.

If my tendency is to think of the glass being half-empty instead of half-full, then I may be a gloomy, negative sort of person. This may have internal consequences affecting my health, fulfilment, happiness and relationships in general to the people and the world around me. There are external consequences, too, in what flows from how people relate to me.

I put my thoughts into action in how I *direct* them at people or situations; in other words, through loving or controlling wishes, or in what I do. In the latter case I come up against the laws and conventions of the environment that I inhabit. If I am caught offending against those laws, etc., I may be condemned by public opinion, fined or imprisoned; and then, of course, that will affect how I think, which in turn will affect what I subsequently do. And so it goes on, until I learn to coordinate my thoughts and actions in such a way that I'm not attempting to occupy anybody else's space on the cosmic jigsaw – or letting anybody try to occupy mine, which can only happen if I allow my thoughts to be controlled.

I know one thing for sure: I never wanted, nor do I want, anybody to tell me how to live my life, which includes the death of my body. I regret very much the extent to which I may not have applied that philosophy and behaviour in my relationships with others. But what's past is past, and all I can do is my best with the continuing present.

I'm reminded of a story of somebody who went to Buddha asking for the secret of enlightenment. He was anticipating an extensive list of answers, but all Buddha said was: 'Do your best.'

The concept of punishment

I wanted to bring up another point with Margaret Anna. I said, 'When you talk about there being no laws or rules or regulations in spirit and, incidentally, no concept of punishment, people would very likely find it hard to imagine how things could be similarly arranged on earth. In spirit you don't have to bother about money or religion or nationalism – the sort of things that people fight about or even kill for. I seem to be getting an impression from you that you'd like to see the way of spirit mirrored on earth in the way we manage our affairs.'

Margaret Anna said, *'Not just me – many of us are focused on that. Putting it simply, we'd like people to be able to enjoy themselves more than they do at present. We know that a way to achieve that would be to create conditions where there would be no need for laws and punishments.*

'On the subject of punishment, if you cast your mind back to when you were going to school, corporal punishment was the order of the day then, wasn't it?'

I didn't have to hesitate before answering, 'Emphatically and often brutally so.' The poor chair-woman raised her head or, I should say, the leg of her chair, again!

Margaret Anna said: *'And it isn't now. The system of education hasn't collapsed because of that change, has it? In fact, it's incomparably better. Teachers don't have to be abusers, nor children victims, as was so often the case. I think we can agree that punishment and the fear it generated never brought out the best in children. It's hardly likely to do so with adults either. After all, what are adults but big children?'*

Life would be very simple if we were all kind and loving towards each other. Some of us are, and some of us aren't. To the extent that we aren't, we're going against our true natures – our divine essence, as my spirit guides emphasised. Sometimes we hurt others by our behaviour. Often we do so unconsciously. Indeed, it seems that it would be impossible – or, at least, highly improbable – that we could get through our lives without doing so. On other occasions we hurt others consciously.

During my talks and workshops I would sometimes suggest to people that they take a few moments to ask themselves how often they acted towards others out of sheer malice. I suggested that the answer would usually be 'never'. Nobody ever disagreed with me. I'm not so naïve as to think that some people don't act out of malice; I would, however, suggest that the majority of people don't.

Margaret Anna described how she reviewed her recent physical lifetime when she had settled into her new life in spirit. She had a complete picture of her achievements and her failings – a snapshot of how she had lived her life. In her overall judgement, she found that she did better than she would have expected because of all the condemnation she had experienced during her life. She was able to forgive herself for her failings, with the result that she could go on to enjoy herself unreservedly.

Even Cyprian's behaviour, extreme as it was, was not unusual in the history of the human race, particularly during such events as the Holy Inquisition, when people 'acting on God's behalf' had no compunction in consigning other people to eternal punishment in Hell by burning them at the stake. That temporary, physical burning was symbolic of the eternal one. Countless crimes against humanity have been committed in the name of God – an easy justification.

I hesitated over including Cyprian's story in this book because of the brutality it portrayed. But I realised that the decision wasn't mine to make. I had agreed to the collaboration with Margaret Anna and she considered it extremely important for us all to understand that we 'make our own beds' by how we use our free will. If we separate ourselves from our true, unconditionally loving natures – and taking into consideration the extent to which we do so – then we can't avoid facing ourselves at some point and finding a way to free ourselves from our separation from our divine essence and, ultimately, to be able to forgive ourselves for our betrayal of our divine natures.

The way that Cyprian chose was personal to him. As he had used his free will in his cruel behaviour towards others, he later used his free will to find his way back from how he had, literally, lost himself. As Margaret Anna confirmed, his way is not intended to be seen as a guideline for others but, rather, as an example of the difficulties people create for themselves.

The idea that we are all part of the animating force of all life – or whatever we call it – is awesome in its magnificence. Personally, I can bring it down to earth, as it were, by using an analogy of a jigsaw puzzle. Each piece of the puzzle is different and no piece can fit into the space that belongs to another piece. Thus each piece is individual and unique – but it's at one with the overall picture, and the picture isn't complete without it. So it is with us. Each of us is individual, with our own special, unique qualities. We can't fit into anybody else's place, nor can anybody else fit into ours. Yet, just as a jigsaw puzzle isn't complete without each piece, neither is the universe complete without each of us in our own place, not interfering with or imposing our will on any others, but ultimately using our free will in complete alignment with unconditional love – in other words, being unconditionally loving in our way of living in the world – which may be too much to hope for while we're still human. All we can do is our best, making due allowance for our humanity.

Chapter 14

Learning from Experience

In my view, Cyprian's story is hugely significant in highlight-ing the recurring cycle of cause and effect – an extreme case that one would hope would be a rare occurrence in the further evolution of human existence. What might seem to be 'humdrum' lives can look much more attractive when seen in the light of a life such as Cyprian's.

When we look back at our lives, though, I imagine that we would wish that we had done some things differently. We may blame ourselves for all sorts of 'sins of omission'. We change imperceptibly throughout our lives, and we realise that we see things differently now than we may have done at earlier peri-ods in our lives. If there are things that we regret – as there are bound to be – perhaps we can see that we were acting out of our states of consciousness, such as they were when the things happened. In any case, we can't change the past, but we can change how we look at it – and then learn from it. Perhaps, then, it's easier to move on without carrying any negative baggage, such as guilt, recriminations and grievances, from the past.

I remember reading a story about two monks – let's call them Ambrose and Ernest – who were walking along by a river. At some stage on their walk they met a young woman who wanted to get across the river. Because there was no bridge, the only way over was to walk. The river was too shallow for swimming, but deep enough to make her nervous about taking the plunge.

Ambrose saw her dilemma and offered to carry her across. She got up on his back and he walked across and deposited her on the other side. Then he went back and rejoined Ernest.

They continued to walk along silently for some time. Then Ernest stopped and said suddenly to Ambrose, 'You committed a serious sin back there.'

'How?' asked Ambrose.

Ernest replied, 'You know we're forbidden to touch a woman, and you carried that woman on your back. You'll carry a burden of guilt for that all your life.'

'Oh no,' said Ambrose. 'I left the woman on the other side of the river, but you've been carrying her on your back ever since. I'm not the one who should be burdened with guilt – you have been eating yourself up judging and condemning me.'

Ernest was continuing to carry negative baggage; Ambrose was free.

In my experience, I have found that many people seem to be harder on themselves than others would be. Margaret Anna has referred to souls being 'hell-bent', in a manner of speaking, on self-punishment. She said, *'The old saying that we're our own worst enemies is indisputably true, as I can now see in a far more comprehensive way than would have been possible for me on earth.'*

An education

Margaret Anna sees education as something that isn't confined to schools or colleges, and not simply a means by which people obtain various kinds of qualifications that enhance their career prospects. All that's fine. What she's thinking about, though, is a process that continues all through people's lives, and, ideally, provides them with a philosophy that gives them an understanding of themselves and their place in the universal scheme of things. All the academic qualifications in the world won't be any use to them when they leave their bodies, as they surely will, if they don't have such an understanding.

She says, *'Everybody is a teacher and everybody is a student. People are constantly teaching, and learning from, each other. Some operate on more public platforms than others – such as professional teachers, writers, media pundits and counsellors. Many highly effective teachers have no formal qualifications at all.'*

I wouldn't like to give an impression that my experience of teachers bore any subsequent similarity to that of my childhood encounter with the 'chair-woman'. That was mercifully confined to less than two years (although it seemed like an eternity). Later on I had a lovely teacher, who happened to be a cousin of mine, who groomed me for scholarships that I could never have got without her. She changed the whole course of my life and I always remember her with deep gratitude.

Apart from the academic side of things, as Margaret Anna has said, everybody we meet going through life teaches us something – although not necessarily intentionally. How people deal with other people and situations in their lives, whether negatively or positively, can help us in our approach to our own experiences.

One of the most inspiring people I have met was a man named Giovanni, who came to see me. As a boy of nine, he was playing in a disused quarry in Italy. He found what seemed to him to be like a ball with a pin out on top of it. He pulled the pin and the ball exploded. It was a grenade, a legacy of the Second World War. He lost both of his eyes, as well as one arm. Instead of being bitter or holding a grievance against God or the world, he was profoundly grateful for the direction that this appalling tragedy gave to his life. Because he couldn't see people, he never made superficial judgements based on their looks. He responded to the *feeling* he got from a person – which, incidentally, helped him a lot in his work as a therapist, a profession that he might not have considered going into had it not been for one instantaneous happening that influenced his life so dramatically. The ripples flowed out into how he was able to see the real person more clearly without any dependence on appearance, and I'm sure many people benefited from meeting him, as I had, and admiring the positivity of his approach to life, including his non-judgementalism.

I also remember with gratitude someone who was very much an unconscious teacher. She was a widowed farmer's wife, who lived near my first family home. She had lived mostly on her own for many years. During my adolescence and teenage years I used to visit her fairly regularly. She always had lemonade and biscuits for me, and we would sit very companionably, gazing into an open fire that she'd make sure to build up until it was very nicely blazing.

Our conversation was desultory and inconsequential, with long, comfortable silences, while the fire threw out its shapes at us. I had no awareness of the passage of time (as it happened, I didn't own a watch at the time anyway) until eventually I'd invariably find myself nodding off to sleep. Then, reluctantly, I'd feel it was time for me to go home.

I can't say in all honesty that my visits to her were for altruistic reasons – in order to keep her company, for example. I just loved visiting her and I like to think that she equally enjoyed my visits. Unconsciously, I learned valuable lessons from her – things like the beauty of silence in communication, and the value of discussion not necessarily being in words spoken, but in the comforting feeling of togetherness that it can inspire. She's long gone now, but maybe I'll visit her again and she'll have lemonade and biscuits waiting for me – with an open fire once again showing us pictures in its flames.

The experience of reincarnation

In her physical life Margaret Anna had devoted much of her energy to trying to achieve social reform. I asked her what social reform means to her now.

She replied, '*Social reform in the sense of improved living conditions for everybody is the end result of raising awareness all round. That means more emphasis on education. That was one of my "babies" when I was last on earth. Primarily, I see education as a means of helping people to open their minds – not a collection of facts, obviously, but a way of thinking. The teachers need to be educated as well as the students.*'

I asked her, 'Given that they have incarnated or reincarnated from a spirit state, how is it that some people believe there's nothing beyond physical existence?'

Margaret Anna replied that the answer came into the sphere of education, as she saw it. The broad picture is that the soul gets a fresh chance, without the encumbrance of remembering previous existence with its incidental traumas. After that it becomes a question of the individual choice of parents, environment, etc. It depends on what a soul has set out to achieve in a particular earth life.

Suppose, for example, I had been a fanatical devotee of a specific religious organisation and not only did I refuse to tolerate any other belief, but I actively persecuted those who did. I might reasonably choose not to have anything to do with religion in a later life, with the aim of freeing myself from my previous obsession.

Then suppose that something, a book I read, say, or a meeting with somebody, presents me with a philosophy of openness and tolerance that appeals to me. I may be receptive to it in a way that I'd never have countenanced in my previous life. Alternatively, maybe I just live out my life as an agnostic or an atheist. I'll probably get a bit of a surprise when I pass on; that, in itself, should be enough to promote some curiosity about my unexpected condition.

I wondered what Margaret Anna meant about teachers needing to be educated. She said that she didn't mean to cast a reflection on teachers in any way. She's well aware of the marvellous work they do. She explained that she wasn't thinking of teachers in an exclusively vocational sense. Her perspective is based on what they – on her side – see as an important part of raising people's awareness. They want to accelerate the whole process so that souls won't continue to be caught in the web of repeating patterns of cause and effect. Apart from their work generally, the guides have been focusing on the elimination of the perceived need for what Margaret Anna might call 'victimhood'. To this end, they'd like to have considerably expanded cooperative arrangements with souls who are at present in physical bodies.

Margaret Anna said that it would break my heart if I saw the state of confusion that many – far from all, thankfully – souls are in when they make the transition from their physical state. Either they're expecting to be put into 'bad boxes' and sent to unimaginable places of punishment, or they have no idea at all what to expect. With souls who are in one or other of those categories, progress is inevitably very slow. When the guides manage to get through to them eventually, they are handicapped by the fact that they are all in spirit.

Margaret Anna said she knew that might sound strange to me. What she meant was that, because what they perceive as their crimes or sins or shortcomings of whatever kind happened on earth, then, once they become aware of the possibility of reincarnation, they are likely to convince themselves that the best place for atonement was back on earth. Not all of them, but a sizeable proportion; in Margaret Anna's view, one is too many.

I was a bit surprised by what she was conveying to me; she seemed to be implying that she wasn't too keen on reincarnation as a means of growth. I checked that out with her.

Margaret Anna explained, *'Looked at from the growth end, I don't think it has been particularly effective so far. The fly in the ointment is how people use their free will. "You can lead a horse to water ..." type of thing.'*

She went on to say, however, that if reincarnation were not a possibility, the guides would have a much harder task to try to get through to souls who are caught in guilt traps. On balance, it's worth the pain and hassle of a self-imposed life as a victim if the soul will then feel free to open itself to enjoying its life in spirit.

Her barometer of the success or failure of reincarnation as a process has to be the levels of pain and suffering on earth. The more that those levels diminish, the happier she is with the process. The guides' aim is that, one day, reincarnation will be seen as a joyful adventure rather than a *via dolorosa*.

Animals as teachers

In seeing education in its widest context, of everybody being a teacher, I was reminded of a time when I was writing about karma – which I suppose I could describe as a sort of log book of our lives showing all their credits and debits. As I was writing, I had a little dog named Misty sitting on my lap. I asked her what she thought about karma. She looked at me with big, loving eyes and licked my hand. What better answer could I have got? She lived totally in the moment and loved unconditionally. That didn't mean that she automatically liked everybody and every situation, but she dealt with them in a completely spontaneous way without subterfuge or contrivance. I thought that if I could be like that – while retaining the benefit of my rational faculties (such as they are!) – the karmic effects could only be positive on the credit side, as it were.

Animals are wonderful teachers, as well as being such loving companions. It's sad to think that a lot of traditional teaching was (and maybe still is) that animals don't have souls. When I hear the word 'having' being applied to souls, I can't help feeling as if I have been locked into a dark cavern, or something like that; it's not a question of 'having' souls but of 'being' souls. Shebaka has explained to me that *all* non-stationary life – in other words, whatever moves – is soul. Stationary life – a rock, for example – is not soul.

I asked Margaret Anna if she had any comments about animals. She did, of course, since they figure prominently on earth. *'They are soul. All souls are part of God. That's it, really. It follows that it's important that they are treated with respect and love.*

'All physical forms are just vehicles for growth in awareness. Picture them all linked together as in a chain, with the human state being at the end of the chain. Each link in the chain is supporting every other link. All the others are moving towards being absorbed into the human state. Until they're ready, it's helpful for them to assist human survival so that, ideally, the humans will progress significantly in their evolution – which in turn will help all the other links in the chain.

'I can tell you that if I were to reincarnate I'd be campaigning actively for animal rights. The fact that there's so much cruelty to animals is a festering wound in human consciousness. Fortunately, there are many people who are working wonders in creating shifts in awareness where animals are concerned. Needless to say, we on this side are helping them in every way we can.

'I have seen many loving reunions between pets and their former owners. These are often totally unexpected and are all the more joyful for that.'

I was reminded of the man who wouldn't accept that he was dead, and woke me up one night when I felt his presence in my bedroom. Although, as I said, he was gone in the morning, he tended to come back sometimes and take up 'residence' on the landing at the top of the stairs. Misty was well aware of him, and used to bark furiously at him. I don't know whether he took any notice of her. He left eventually, and I hope he's reconciled to, and maybe happy in, his situation now.

My reason for mentioning him again is to draw attention to the fact that dogs and cats (I don't know about other animals, but I assume the same thing applies) can see spirit beings much more readily than humans can. My understanding is that cats provide great protection against negative energy, such as a bigoted, closed-minded environment. I don't know how it works, but this is what I've been told. Dogs are, of course, notoriously protective of their owners and never seem to hold grudges, even when they're badly treated, as they often are. Cruelty to animals simply doesn't bear thinking about.

Some people think that cats aren't affectionate, as dogs are. Cats don't show their affection as demonstrably as dogs do and – although this is only my opinion – their owners may need to show that they are worthy of their cats' affection before it will be bestowed. I use the word 'bestow' because I think that cats have a sort of regal quality about them, which demands recognition and respect from their so-called owners. Cats usually choose their owners, as distinct from dogs, who perhaps are generally more trusting of human nature.

It's well known that animals make a big difference when they are allowed to live in nursing homes and interact with the residents. They bring a lot of joy into the lives of people who are confined to institutional existence.

I'm always filled with wonder at how guide dogs manage their 'charges'. It's an interesting comparison to how our spirit guides operate. One of the participants in a course that I ran used to bring a lovely, retired guide dog with him. Everybody on the course loved him. He just lay quietly on the floor, adding his calm presence to the whole proceedings. Incidentally, his owner told me that, once his harness was removed, he reverted to acting like a normal dog – 'off duty', as it were.

There are many stories of how other animals, notably dolphins, interact with humans in a playful way. In general, too, animals respond beautifully to consideration and kindness on the part of humans. They teach us a lot, if we're willingly to learn; above all, perhaps, about love.

Misty was a 'chocoholic'. She once ate a whole box of chocolates that had been mistakenly left on the dining-room floor. She didn't seem to suffer any negative reaction from them. She had survived more than two years longer than the usual lifespan for her breed (King Charles Spaniel), and she no longer had any quality of life. She couldn't use her hind legs to get up from the floor, and it became pitiful to see her lying so helplessly. After agonising heart-searching, we felt we had to let her go. We gave her as happy an exit as we could by feeding her chocolate while the final injection was being administered. I haven't actually seen her since, but I have often felt her presence in the house.

Margaret Anna's description of the loving reunions between owners and their pets is very consoling. I have met many people who were deeply distressed at the loss of their beloved 'friends', who had made no demands on them, other than for food and affection, and who gave so much love unreservedly. Sometimes the loss of a pet affects its human owner more than that of a relative or friend – partly because they feel they can't grieve so openly for what some people dismiss as 'just' animals.

It always pains me when I hear a person's behaviour being described as 'like an animal'. Animals never behave in as deliberately cruel a manner as some humans do.

When animals die

Many people ask what happens to animals when they die. My guide Shebaka provided a good answer to this question.

He said, *'It may be helpful if we take an example of, say, a dog that becomes ill and dies. Its guide helps it through the transition in such a way that it is not, in fact, aware of the transition for some time – the equivalent of a day or so in your time. This period of rest (like sleep) is necessary so that the mental effects of the illness will be overcome. When it becomes conscious, it is still in the non-material equivalent of its physical body, but without infirmity of any kind.*

'The first sensation it feels is hunger, and immediately a dish of its favourite food appears before it. The thought of the food produces it; the power of thought in actualising itself is much more obvious in spirit than it is on earth. Of course, the power itself is not less on earth – its effects are less obvious. Food is not necessary for survival in spirit and, of course, its substance is not material, but neither is the substance of the spirit body. What is produced as food can be just as real, and as palatable, to the spirit body as material food is to the physical body.

'When its hunger is satisfied, the dog's next thought is of its people, who are themselves thinking of it and grieving over its passing. No sooner thought than done; the dog is immediately with them. They can feel its presence if they don't reason themselves out of the feeling – or if they are aware enough to recognise it. It's possible for its guide to communicate with the dog in such a way that it realises that its people cannot see it and therefore cannot show their love for it in the same way as they did while it was in its physical body. It will know that its owners still love it as much as ever. It stays with its people, and comes and goes to them as long as both sides need the contact.'

I'm informed that all forms of animal life – not just dogs – are looked after by guides when they die. Frank has told me that Misty is enjoying herself immensely. Her passing left a huge void in my life but, as I have said earlier, I have felt her presence in many ways since she passed on. For example, when I have been out somewhere, and I'm opening the door to enter my home, I can feel her waiting behind the door as she always did. That doesn't happen as often as it did earlier on, just after her passing, so I presume she's getting on with enjoying herself.

Shebaka has provided me with great insight into our relationship with animals, and it's something that's worth considering when we look at our evolutionary path: *'Many people are cruel to animals because they don't understand that they are also souls. Cruelty is often described as mindlessness; I can't think of a more apt description, given that mind is soul. Cruelty is a negation of soul to the extent that it obscures the loving nature of soul. I include all forms of cruelty, both physical and mental – although, of course, all cruelty is, in fact, mental. There are obvious forms of cruelty, such as torture, or what are known as blood sports, but there are many less obvious ones such as abandonment or neglect of dependent creatures. Cruelty may often result in nothing more negative than mere thoughtlessness. Whatever its manifestations or apparent consequences, the perpetrator of cruelty ultimately causes most damage to himself, to his own awareness. Neither the hare that is pursued and mangled by dogs, nor the dogs who do the pursuing and mangling, are likely to be damaged to anything like the same extent as the organisers and participants in the event.'*

Being kind to animals is just one of the lessons that it's important for us to learn on our evolutionary path. The benefits that accrue to us from showing such kindness are immeasurable. We're rewarded with companionship, demonstrable affection and unconditional acceptance, no matter how we are.

Chapter 15

Love Never Fails

When Margaret Anna announced that she was going to tell me another story, I sat in eager anticipation, with pen poised. Margaret Anna's method of illustrating things by telling stories appealed to me very much. I hadn't a clue what to expect from her story. That made the unfolding of it all the more interesting for me – rather like reading a book without knowing how the plot was going to develop.

Margaret Anna's story had its origins in the sixteenth century, during the reign of King Henry VIII in England. A young man named Stephen has set his heart on becoming a priest, but he's in a dilemma. In spite of himself, Stephen has fallen in love. Her name is Catherine, and she returns his love. After much agonising, he decides that Catherine has come into his life as a test of the strength of his vocation and that what's required of him is to sacrifice his human love for the greater glory of God.

Although she's heartbroken, Catherine can only accept his decision. Stephen is duly ordained as a priest and settles into his duties.

Martin Luther is assuming a public profile and what became known as the Reformation is getting under way. King Henry, initially, and his Chancellor, Sir Thomas More, are defenders of the established Church with the Pope as its head. There's much to-ing and fro-ing of arguments and diatribes. None of this is of any immediate concern to Stephen. There's no radio or television to keep him informed of what's going on. He gets on with his work as best he can.

In the meantime, a marriage has been arranged for Catherine by her parents. She hasn't forgotten Stephen, but she adapts herself as wholeheartedly as she can to her life as it's now unfolding.

Time passes. One day Stephen is called urgently to the bedside of a dying woman. To his horror, he finds that it's Catherine, whom he hasn't seen – and has tried to forget – for many years. She's still conscious. All the feeling that both of them had tried to suppress comes to the surface. He has to remind himself to give her the last rites. She dies holding his hand.

Stephen rails against the cruel fate (as he sees it) that forced him to make a choice between his vocation and Catherine. He tells himself that if he had married her she would never have got the infection that took her still-young life.

In due course he hears about the religious developments. Those who are following Luther's line are regarded as heretics and are liable to be tortured or put to death by burning if they don't recant. Stephen is now in a rebellious frame of mind and open to the new teaching. He becomes part of an underground network which aims to spread the new 'gospel'. Unfortunately for him, spies are everywhere and he's exposed. He's severely tortured and eventually recants. A broken and disillusioned man, his health fails and he dies a few short years later.

The scene shifts to Ireland in the nineteenth century. It's a time of hope, much of it inspired by the Liberator, Daniel O'Connell. A young couple, Ruairi and Maureen, childhood sweethearts, are due to get married. Then comes the Great Famine to blight all of their crops and their hopes. There's a place for one of them to go to the land of opportunity, America. After much persuasion from Ruairi Maureen agrees to go first, with Ruairi to follow later, as soon as he is able to. He wants Maureen to be safe; whether he'll be able to follow her is uncertain in the prevailing conditions.

There's heartbreak once again as Maureen leaves. Hope turns to despair for Ruairi, as blight follows blight, starvation takes its toll and he becomes one of the many victims of the famine.

Maureen survives and, after many hardships, becomes a teacher. She helps many children of those Irish emigrants who managed to negotiate the journey to America and all the vicissitudes of settling into a new culture. Eventually she gives up hope of meeting Ruairi again. She doesn't marry, although it's not for want of offers. Much respected, she dies some thirty years after leaving Ireland.

Now we move to the present century. Robert is a psychiatrist living in America. He was married with two children but now, in his mid-50s, he is divorced. He has recently taken on a new client, a twice-married and divorced woman named Freda. She was born in Ireland, but has lived in America for the past forty years – since her parents emigrated when she was only five. She has one daughter by her first marriage and two sons by her second. She is now a grandmother. For the past seven months she has been living with a man who is pressing her to marry him, but after two failed marriages she's hesitant about accepting his proposals. She's also not sure about her feelings for him.

After a few sessions with Freda, Robert is in an ethical dilemma. He realises that he has fallen in love with her. While he has been increasingly looking forward to his meetings with her, he decides that he has no choice but to discontinue seeing her and to refer her to a colleague.

Freda, too, has been struggling with her feelings for Robert. She tells herself that this is par for the course for him – that she's just one of many women who imagine that they're in love with him. She resolves not to fall into that trap. She has been coming to the conclusion that maybe it would be better if she stopped seeing him, when he tells her that he's calling a halt to their sessions. She's very disappointed, but at the same time relieved. She doesn't want to have any more emotional turmoil in her life and, in her view, she would certainly be putting herself in the way of it by continuing to see him.

Time passes and they both get on with their lives. She's still in her relationship, but refusing to commit herself to marriage. He has had a brief affair, which had ended by mutual consent.

One day he's passing a bookshop, when he gets an urge to go in. He's arguing with himself that he has no time at present to indulge his love for books, but he still responds to the urge.

Inside the bookshop he suddenly comes face to face with Freda. Their pleasure at seeing each other is spontaneous. Even though he realises that he's going to be late for an appointment, he invites her to have coffee with him. She accepts. They enjoy each other's company enormously.

Margaret Anna says, *'I hardly need to fill you in on the rest of the story. It is love realised and fulfilled. Released from the burden of being her therapist, he is able to be himself in all his humanity. She, in turn, sees that to him she's an attractive woman rather than a client. They literally fall into each other's arms, and I can say in true romantic parlance that they live happily ever after.*

'You have gathered, of course, that what I've been outlining are episodes from the evolutionary journeys of two souls. In human terms, the first two episodes have tragic outcomes, while the third one ends happily.'

Margaret Anna said that she wanted to tell me this story partly because she's a romantic at heart, but mainly to show how free will and conditioning intertwine and often interfere with the flow of love. Stephen was caught within the cage of his rigid beliefs. In the case of Ruairi and Maureen, they were physically separated because of their decision (which was mainly Ruairi's) that Maureen should go ahead of him to America – an understandable decision under the circumstances. When they again appeared as Freda and Robert, their coming together was delayed until relatively late in their lives. But, in the end, love found a way to clear all the hurdles.

Margaret Anna commented, *'A sceptic might say that it was just a coincidence that Robert happened to get the urge to go into the bookshop at the very time that Freda was there. But it wasn't. Guides are always on the look-out for such opportunities. People often ignore their nudges, but the guides never give up.'*

Margaret Anna stressed that it was important to say that, on their separate journeys, both souls would have been seeking to resolve other aspects of their evolutionary debits, including the karmic effects accruing to other relationships.

Ruairi punished himself for his rejection of Catherine when he was Stephen, and he sought to compensate by ensuring that Maureen – the 'resurrected' Catherine – would have an opportunity for survival and freedom from hardship. In the third episode Robert could again have been caught in a vocational trap, as he had (as Stephen) been in the first.

That story was very different from any of Margaret Anna's other stories. It's a love story spanning six centuries, and the 'stars' of the story had to go through tragic separation before they finally found themselves free to express their love for each other – in circumstances that allowed them complete freedom to be together.

I remarked to Margaret Anna that it was third time lucky for them.

'Except that luck didn't enter into it,' she said.

I commented on the fact that in each of the episodes the lovers were in the same gender relationship with each other. I asked her if that was usual.

She replied, *'That was their choice. It's always up to the souls them-selves how they want to act out their evolution. I would wish that the fragment of the evolution of two souls that I outlined would be seen as a message of hope. Maybe things don't work out in one lifetime, but they will in another.'*

The prospect of reincarnation – or even life together in spirit – is comforting. But do we want to wait? I said to Margaret Anna, 'The trouble is that, with all our advances in technology and so on, we want "quick fixes". From my own experience, I know that people don't like to be told that they might have to wait a year or two for something that they want to happen – let alone a lifetime or two or three!'

Margaret Anna said, *'I was a prime example of impatience in action myself. Many people, admittedly inadvertently, tried to teach me patience by withholding their approval of my plans. But I wasn't very responsive, so the lessons kept being repeated over and over. I was full of how much I wanted to get done – and how little time I might have, particularly because of my ill-health. Later, I realised that it was enough for me to sow seeds. Others would be there to reap the harvest.*

'I'm using myself as an example because I want people to know that, although my life on earth as Margaret Anna was sprayed with disillusionment and rejections, now I'm as happy as can be.'

One might well ask why the lovers didn't just reunite in spirit after the first episode, and not bother having to go through all the harrowing experiences of the ensuing lives. It's all a matter of free will, of course – as Margaret Anna has stressed repeatedly – and it was their own choice. In having dealt with other karmic issues in their evolution, they could reach out to each other finally within the physical framework, clear of all negative baggage.

A celibate life

I had been forming an impression from some of our conversations that Margaret Anna wasn't in favour of celibacy as a way of life on earth. I thought I had better seek clarification so I asked her was I making a fair deduction.

Margaret Anna said that the impression that I was getting only related to prescribed celibacy. She elaborated, *'If people are voluntarily celibate, that's how they're expressing their free will. Anything that's imposed is contrary to the way of spirit.'*

I remarked that some people may not *want* to be celibate, but don't have any opportunity to be otherwise.

She replied, *'There could be all sorts of reasons for that. It's probable that it's in accordance with their soul purpose. For example, they may feel that they had indulged themselves obsessively in sexual activity in previous lives and want to balance the scales.'*

Making choices

I think I can understand why souls want to work things out on earth, even though they know they're going to be inflicting a lot of punishment on themselves. I'm sure I chose to do that myself – although I don't think I'll make that choice again. Before I go this time, I want to make certain that I'm not going to leave any unfinished business that I might feel compelled to come back to sort out. In saying that, I don't want to imply that this lifetime has been an unhappy experience for me. Rather the reverse; I have had many sadnesses and fears, some of which I have outlined in this book, but I have also had many wonderful experiences, including, of course, all the communication I have been privileged to have had with spirit collaborators. I have also met countless marvellous people. But I'll be renewing 'old' friendships and I won't be saying goodbye to anybody.

If Stephen had followed his heart in the first lifetime, there wouldn't have been any need for the others, unless he had found other reasons for reincarnating. But that's easy to say. When his conditioned thinking is taken into account, it can be seen that he felt he had no choice but to act as he did. The moral is, of course, not to let ourselves be controlled by rigidity of thinking. We need to take heed of what our hearts tell us, and open up the analytical cages to which we have become accustomed.

Most people are probably familiar with what's called a *déjà vu* type of experience, which is described in my dictionary as 'an illusory feeling of having already experienced a present situation'. Apart from the use of the word 'illusory', this seems to me to be a good description. Personally, I'd view the experience as an instantaneous memory of having met somebody, heard something or been somewhere before, while knowing that that didn't happen in the present lifetime. As far as I'm concerned, the explanation is simple enough; it's a flash of a fragment of a previous life.

The only time I was in Brussels I was in a large shop when I suddenly became aware of a woman standing at a distance. We looked at each other simultaneously and smiled. It wasn't a 'some enchanted evening across a crowded room' sort of thing; it was just a smile and then we went on with our business. I'm sure many people will have had that type of experience; it's like an acknowledgement of familiarity.

Something that I observed with wonder when I was doing individual consultations was that sometimes a number of people would come in 'clusters'. They were people who didn't know each other in this life, but who shared similar types of experiences in past lives. They didn't come to see me specifically to hear about past lives. That type of information would have emerged in the course of general readings. It just so happened that, completely independently of each other, they made appointments that followed each other more or less sequentially.

The most common type of cluster involved people who, according to information that I received, had been Cathars, mainly in the south of France. They rejected the beliefs of the orthodox Church; they professed total equality of souls ('no hierarchy or structure, for no one is greater than another'); and the notion of Hell was an absurdity as far as they were concerned. Women had equal status with men (something for which Margaret Anna worked so hard later on). In a series of crusades ordered by Pope Innocent III, the Cathars were brutally exterminated during the thirteenth century with, apparently, the last of them having been burned at the stake at Montsegur, Languedoc, in 1244.

Again, one might well ask why people who had gone through such a horrific experience – being burned at the stake – would choose to undergo another physical experience. I think the answer might be related to a prophecy left by the

Cathars – that what they called the 'church of love' would be proclaimed in 1986. There was no such obvious happening in that year, but certainly there has been a significant raising of consciousness in the latter part of the twentieth century, and, indeed, this one. In my view, it's likely that they're involved in that.

There's an expression that I often heard used: 'It was like somebody walking over my grave.' This also seems to apply to a sudden past-life memory, causing us to shiver or start. I'm sure most people will have experienced a feeling of already knowing somebody that they're meeting for the first time – a feeling that's sometimes articulated by questions, such as, 'Where have I met you before?'

In any case, going back to Margaret Anna's story, I feel that it's heart-warming, and we can rejoice in its happy ending. She reminds us that, irrespective of how much we resist it through our conditioned behaviour, love will find a way to clear all obstacles to its full expression – even if it takes many centuries in our time to reach that haven.

Chapter 16

About Brian

In a seemingly strange coincidence of timing I had got involved in writing this book when, on 9 August 2009, my son Brian died at the age of 46. I felt it important to include his story in the book, partly because of the immediacy of its relevance to the subject matter of the book, but also because, in a way that I'll explain, it brought my beliefs full circle from my concerns about my father, as I described earlier, to those about my son.

Margaret Anna's communications did much to diminish the trauma associated with the death experience. While she very much respected the sadness of the separation caused by it, she presented death as something joyous – a reunion of sorts – and this was something that brought me great comfort.

Brian was a bachelor and lived on his own. Although he had never played football, he had an abiding interest in collecting and collating statistics about it, so it would have been like the end of his world if he had been deprived of his computer. I discovered after his death that some of his friends had nick-named him 'Stats', and his support for the local football team – Bohemians – was legendary. In thirty-one years he missed only two home matches.

For many years Brian had had a rather inconspicuous lump on his right hand, and it had not even cost him a thought. In 2005 he was alarmed to see that the lump had become purple in colour, and was persuaded to get medical attention. An investigation led to the diagnosis of melanoma, followed by complicated and lengthy surgery resulting in the amputa-tion of most of his hand. He learned to write quite well with his left hand and to use his computer proficiently. He was able to carry on with his life much as before, and all seemed well.

In fact, the medical team who looked after Brian expressed confidence that the surgery had removed the cancer. However, early in 2008 tests showed that the cancer hadn't been elimi-nated but had reached a terminal stage.

Brian took the news philosophically. He said that he already knew what the prognosis would be. He took part in an exper-imental programme of treatment, which included chemo-therapy. When tests showed that there was no improvement, he opted out of any further treatment, but agreed to weekly atten-dance at the day centre of Blackrock Hospice in County Dublin. He continued to live independently without any hint of complaint or self-pity.

For me, this was an extremely challenging period of my life. It brought back to me all of the fears that I'd had about my father, and I was overwhelmed by the memories I had of our farewell. I remembered clearly the distress I felt that I had not been able to talk to him about my deep love for him, my fears for his eternal future, and the respect and gratitude I had for the way he had lived his life. Although I no longer feared death in the same way that I had as a child and a young man, I was torn by the prospect of Brian's death. Superficially, I was back to an ironic sameness about my situation in that I knew I was leaving my dying father and now waiting to say farewell to my dying son, who also had abandoned all religious practice.

Whenever he was asked about his beliefs, Brian's reply had always been direct and unambiguous. He was very much of the 'when you're dead, you're dead' school of thinking. Of course hellfire was no longer a dragon to be feared, and my approach to life and death had changed dramatically since the death of my father. At the same time, however, I was deeply concerned about the state of confusion that Brian would inevitably find himself in if he passed on believing that there would be only oblivion.

Brian tolerated my beliefs that life would continue after death, and that we have guardian angels available to help us on our paths in this world, but he never showed any great interest in examining them further. He requested and received a copy of each of the eleven books I had published, but, as far as I know, he did not read them. I made no attempt to persuade him to do so.

And so I waited. There will always be situations that cause us worry, and I imagine that it would be very difficult – if not impossible – to go through life on earth without worrying. It has, however, been communicated to me over and over and over again – by Margaret Anna and each and every one of the other guides – that worry is no help to anyone. Worry causes anxiety for the worrier *and* the object of worry.

From the time that I accepted this philosophy, I got into the habit of handing over to my spirit guides the things I simply couldn't handle. Margaret Anna was a particular friend in that department, and I often asked for her help in finding solutions. I understood that in the handing-over process I was aligning myself with the total universal flow of uncon-ditional love. The snag was, and is, of course, that it would be no use doing that if I didn't trust completely in the process; if I didn't, I'd soon find myself back in the worrying mould.

Brian's illness and impending death put my philosophy to the test in an extreme way. His condition was deteriorating and it became more and more obvious that time was running out for him. There seemed to be no inclination on his part to have the type of discussion that I was hoping for. I had done all the handing-over part – and continued to maintain my trust in it – but there was a little niggle that maybe my experience with my father would repeat itself. For the first time in years I felt that same old terror, even though I had faith that my life was very different now and that universal, unconditional love would prevail.

At last, about three months before he died, Brian said he'd like to talk to me about things that were on his mind. He seemed to have moved from his mantra of 'when you're dead, you're dead' to wondering what would happen to him after his body succumbed to the cancer. I explained to him that my understanding was that life continued, and that the key to *how* it would continue lay in our ability to be open-minded. If we're not confined by rigid belief systems, then we can enjoy the adventure of life as it evolves without, for example, illness or any disability. We are given the freedom to explore our own creativity in whatever directions we wish, without restrictions of any kind. He seemed to accept and, more accurately I think, to *know* that he could safely change his mantra to 'when you're dead, you're not dead'. I asked him to let me know after his passing how he was getting on.

'How will you know?' he asked.

I said I'd just know; I'd feel his presence. I also told him that I believed that he'd be able to continue to go to see Bohemians playing if he wished to do so.

I can't even begin to describe how relieved I was after that discussion. The impetus had to come from Brian himself – in his own time and his own way.

Early in July Brian conceded that he couldn't manage by himself any more. He was relieved to be taken into the hospice where he received indescribably loving care during the final weeks of his life.

I was comforted by the thought of Brian's life ending in such loving circumstances. I was equally comforted by my friend Frank.

Frank had already mentioned that he's now part of a sort of welcoming committee for souls leaving their bodies. On 11 July Frank predicted that Brian would pass on in four weeks – which was precisely what happened (on 9 August). Frank promised to have a group ready and waiting to receive Brian with a great welcome. I didn't tell Brian about Frank's prediction on the timing of his death, but I told him about Frank, whom he had never met, and that he was organising a big welcome for him. Brian liked that idea.

Throughout the rest of July and into August, Brian became increasingly weaker. The wonderful hospice staff made sure that he was as comfortable and as free from pain as he could possibly be. As I sat by his bed, I remembered how I used to have to spend hours by his cot trying to get him to go to sleep. If I slipped out of the room at all, he'd wake up crying. Now, there I was sitting by his bed for hours, waiting for him to go to a sleep of a different kind. I wasn't exempt in any way from the sadness of the situation. Images came flooding into my mind of Brian as a child – the years of watching him growing up. I remembered how he kept throwing his toys out of his cot so that I'd have to keep giving them back to him; I recalled his quirky sense of humour – and how his smile lit up his whole countenance. I found it difficult to come to terms with the fact that I wouldn't be visiting him in his apartment any more. Yet through it all I was greatly comforted by the knowledge of the welcome that was waiting for him.

My wife, Phyllis, Brian's mother, had passed away in 2005. After her passing she had let me know that she was enjoying herself immensely, exploring her artistic creativity and meeting with her parents, other relatives and close friends who had predeceased her. In the hospice, shortly before Brian left I felt her presence strongly and had a visual impression of her smiling radiantly and appearing as she had been in her prime in her earthly life. Brian subsequently told me that he had a loving reunion with her.

Of his immediate family, the only ones left were Brian's sister, my daughter, Aisling, and myself. As it so happened, on the day he finally stopped breathing I had left the room for a lunch break. Aisling, who was with him, called me urgently, but by the time I got back he was gone. Sadly, this time, I thought, he didn't wake up crying. Happily, I believe, he woke up laughing.

After Brian's passing, he quickly communicated that he had arrived safely. I had arranged that his body would be taken from the hospice to a funeral home near where I live. After all that was done, when I was on my way home, I felt his presence. He seemed to be very pleased that he had no trouble getting through to me – almost as if he was using his mobile phone – and that Frank's welcoming party had worked out. He told me that while his body was still on his bed in the hospice awaiting the arrival of the undertakers he saw a fly landing on his nose. I had seen that, too, as I was sitting beside the bed – although I had forgotten about it until he reminded me of it. It was only a trivial happening, of course, and it obviously was of no concern to him other than as a simple way of showing me that he was really communicating with me.

Brian had specified precisely the type of funeral that he wanted. I like to think, and I'm sure I'm right, that he did so in the mental security of knowing that he was moving on to a joyful adventure. He wanted his funeral to be a celebratory occasion. He had decided that he wanted his body to be cremated and his ashes placed in a wall with a plaque at Mount Jerome Cemetery in Harold's Cross, Dublin. The funeral was held at the crematorium. About a hundred people packed the small building. He had selected the music he wanted to have played – 'Enter Sandman' (Metallica), 'Freebird' (Lynyrd Skynyrd) and 'Flight of Icarus' (Iron Maiden).

'Are those your favourite pieces?' I asked.

'No,' said Brian, with a quiet smile. 'But they are the pieces that are most appropriate for my funeral.'

The ceremony concluded with the final words from 'The Flight of Icarus'.

It was all done as he wished and, for me, it was a beautifully moving experience. Others who were present told me that it was for them, too, even some who were pleasantly surprised in spite of the lack of religious ritual, which would normally have been important for them.

These days, when I feel that I'm receiving communication from somebody in the spirit world, I usually ask for some little evidence, no matter how mundane, that it's not my imagination taking over. A week after he passed on, I was sitting in Brian's apartment when I felt his presence very clearly. After a little chat I made my usual request for evidence. He conveyed to me that Bohemians, who were due to play a match two days later, would win by two goals. They did. He still had his eye on the ball – just from a different perspective.

Frank conveyed to me that Brian now had a computer, the like of which we couldn't imagine, so that he had no trouble recreating all his statistics. Frank also said that in due course Brian would help with his welcoming group.

The long, drawn-out nature of Brian's illness was a challenging test for me in trusting in the validity of the communications that I have been receiving and writing about for years. I hope that Brian's story will be consoling, particularly for those who may have suffered the loss of loved ones.

Now that it's clear that Brian is enjoying himself in his revived exploration of life, I don't propose to continue contacting him. I want him to enjoy his new situation without interruption. OK, maybe I will just check on him every now and then – but only if he so wishes. It's enough for me to know that he's happy.

Chapter 17

There Are No Goodbyes

One thing that has become abundantly clear in my conversations with Margaret Anna is the fact that anything we consider possible on earth is much more easily achievable in spirit. Consider, for example, something like sport, which is an overwhelming passion for so many people on earth. It used to be predominantly a male type of activity; however, that's increasingly no longer the case. Accordingly, it's hugely important that such an absorbing interest should be capable of being pursued in the spirit realm.

I have already mentioned how, after he had passed on, my son Brian correctly predicted that his football team, Bohemians, would win a particular match by two goals. That reminded me of a prediction I had, many years ago, from a friend of mine, Eileen, who was giving me a call from spirit. She told me that the County Clare hurling team would win an All-Ireland Final by two points. I looked at the match on television, and Clare were being beaten as the final whistle was within a couple of minutes of being blown. I began to doubt the authenticity of my conversation with Eileen; however, in the end, her prediction proved to be accurate.

As has been outlined in the book, one of the big differences between life on earth and life in spirit is that we humans exist within a linear time scale – with a past, present and future. In spirit there is simply a continuing present. In that context it's fairly understandable that souls in spirit can see what our future is – within the canvas of a continuing present. However, it's less easy to understand, I think, how they can enjoy participating in something like sport themselves – whether as spectators or players – if they already know the results.

I have been able to sort out that conundrum satisfactorily for myself. Suppose I want to see a particular match but, for some reason, I'm not free to do so at the time it's being played. I can arrange to have the match recorded so that I can see it whenever it suits me to do so. In the meantime I make sure that I don't know the result. I can then look at the recorded version as if it's happening while I'm looking at it.

In a somewhat similar way, I imagine that souls in spirit can easily create a sort of temporary linear time structure to enable them to have the thrill of participation in the way they enjoyed on earth; that's if they wish to do so, of course.

As a child, Brian had prophetic gifts. When I asked him how he knew certain things, he said that he saw them written on his forehead with a brown line under them. Since his passing he has made predictions, such as the one about the football match, and others that were also accurate, so he seems to have recovered the aptitude that had become obscured as he grew up.

Incidentally, when Brian was on earth he was obsessed with time to an extent bordering on fanaticism. Whenever we arranged to meet he always had to know the precise time that we would do so. He would invariably be one of the first to arrive at football matches. Three days after he was discharged from hospital following major surgery, he insisted that he would have to go to see Bohemians play. Since I couldn't persuade him not to go, I felt I had to accompany him. On a cold, wet November evening we arrived at the ground even before the entrance stiles were open. As the fans arrived, I was struck by the camaraderie that existed between them; many of them made an effort to come and shake Brian's undamaged left hand.

According to Frank, Brian is now associating with a group of other souls (Frank refers to them as his 'charges'), some of whom have similar interests to himself. To the amusement of the other members of the group, Brian kept continually trying to tie their discussions or activities down to time. It seems that coming to terms with a concept of timelessness has been one of his most difficult learning experiences; a nice lesson to have to learn, I imagine.

A participant in a course I was running told a story of two friends, Tom and Joe, whose abiding passion was football – in their youth as players, and, as they grew older, as spectators. In one of their discussions they wondered what life after death might be like. Without reservation, they agreed on one thing – if there was no football in the 'afterlife' it would be a terrible state of affairs. They promised each other that whoever went first would come back to tell the other how he was and, most important, what the position was about football.

In due course, Tom passed on. One Friday night, not long afterwards, Joe was sitting watching television when he suddenly became aware of Tom standing beside him. He didn't see him – he just felt Tom's presence. Joe was startled.

Tom said, 'What are you frightened about? Didn't I promise you I'd come back to fill you in?'

Joe stuttered, 'I know, but … Tell me quick – what's it like? And what about football?'

Tom replied, 'Well, there's good news – and what you might think is not-so-good news. Which do you want to hear first?'

Joe thought for a minute. Then he said, 'I'll have the good news first.'

Tom said, 'It's a wonderful place; you can have anything you like.'

Joe could hardly contain himself.

'But *what about football?*' he nearly shouted.

Tom sighed. 'There's no end of it,' he exclaimed. 'What's more, I'm able to play again – and better than I ever could before.'

Joe was waiting for more, but Tom was silent.

Then Joe blurted out, 'But you said there was not-so-good news.'

Tom was quiet for a moment, and then he said, 'You're on our team next Wednesday.'

That little story, although told as a joke, highlights the fact that, in spite of all the assurances Joe had got about how great things were in spirit, he might not be too anxious to join his friend. I think that's generally the position for many of us.

Speaking for myself, I want to hang on here for another while, even though life would be much easier for me without the physical constraints of old age. I think we all know in our hearts that we have chosen to be born into physical life for special reasons peculiar to ourselves, and that we don't want to leave until we have completed whatever it was we came to do. Colloquially, that can be expressed as going 'when our number's up'. There's also, of course, the fact that we might be intrigued and even excited by what's to come, but it still remains the 'unknown', and that's not always something that we're 'dying' to explore.

Of course, it's hard to understand, from a purely physical standpoint, why some people die young, suddenly, violently, in great pain, in advanced stages of senility, or in any other uncomfortable way. That's only explainable in terms of a soul's evolution, and its own choices as it progresses in that evolution. It's inadvisable – at the very least – to try to make individual judgements. From an earthly point of view, we may not understand the reasons, but we can only trust in the fact that each soul *has* a reason.

The main objects of this book are to eliminate fear of death, to show what life in spirit is like, which means, incidentally comparing it with life on earth, and, as far as possible, to make life easier and more enjoyable for all of us going through physical experiences.

I have no intention of running the risk of boring any reader by going back over material already covered in the book. However, at the same time, I feel that it may be helpful if I highlight certain aspects of what we've discussed, even though doing so may involve some repetition.

The whole course of my life changed when I 'met' Margaret Anna. At the outset, being unaware of who she had been in her last physical life was probably an advantage for me; I had no preconceived opinions about her, and nothing but interest and intrigue. Finding out more about her and her international status as a pioneering spirit for social reform and peace was eye-opening, and it made me conscious of how honoured I was to have her as a spirit guide. Later, when she asked me to collaborate with her in writing this book, I felt more honoured still.

My experiences of writing with Margaret Anna and working with the people who came to me for individual consultations could not be more different. In the latter instance, I always had definite proof from the people concerned that the communications I passed on were accurate and valid. With Margaret Anna, not only was I reliant upon my own belief and sense of trust, but I was entering into philosophical territory that was not readily subject to 'proof'.

Throughout the process, I continually questioned myself. And while there was never even a hint of impatience coming from Margaret Anna, I could often feel her smiling at me with good humour – urging me to forget my doubts and trust my feelings about the material that she was conveying to me.

At one stage, later on in the writing of the book, she could see that I had satisfied myself about my doubts.

She said, *'How do you know whether what I'm saying is true, particularly when it seems to be contrary to so much religious teaching? You haven't any proof, that's for sure – any more than you have proof that I am who I say I am, or even that I'm there at all.'*

I said that, as far as I was personally concerned, I didn't have any doubts, and that I wouldn't have persevered with the book if I had experienced any continuing doubts. However, I could not help but wonder if my own certainty would be of much help to a reader.

I hadn't really answered her question.

She repeated it with more emphasis, saying, *'How do you know, when you haven't any physical evidence?'* Margaret Anna emphasised the word 'know'.

I replied, 'I just *know*. That's the only answer I can give.'

She said, 'That's it – a **knowing** that reaches beyond all analysis. It comes when people are ready. It's as if a light inside them has been switched on.

'It's no different in spirit, which people might find surprising. The closed mind works equally effectively in that state – as does the open one. Admittedly, I have an advantage over you in that I can see you and you can't see me – except vaguely, as you sometimes have said – so that you have to take me more on trust than I you. But when it comes to seeing God, we're both in the same boat – we're seeing God around us all the time in every soul with whom we come into contact.'

I suggested (I was tempted to say 'I know' but I thought I'd better not start getting dogmatic!) that perhaps all people have that 'knowing' that Margaret Anna mentioned. At certain stages in our lives we're all faced with situations or decisions that stretch us in every way. Yet, no matter how much our own analytical processes (or the well-meaning advice we receive from others) point us in one direction, we somehow know that this is not the way that we should go. We may not be able to give any logical reason for *how* we know, but we have gone beyond analysis. Sometimes, of course, we don't follow the path of the 'knowing' and, more than likely, we regret that afterwards.

Handing over

The fact that all people, without exception, have spirit guides – guardian angels, if you like – available to help them, subject to their agreement, was hugely significant and comforting for me.

In this book I have described in detail how I have worked with guides over the past thirty years or so, and I have included suggestions about how people can develop their own methods of communication – if they so wish, and according to their own styles. In my case, I have come to the conclusion that the easiest and ultimately most effective way of working with my guides is to hand over to them problems or challenges for which I can find no ready-made solutions, and to trust that answers will emerge. I cannot verbalise how these answers have so often been a source of wonder – often beyond the scope of any analytical procedures that I might have been inclined to use, and on which I might have wasted a lot of energy.

I must stress, however, that there is nothing passive about the handing-over process. The outcome may involve a lot more activity than might otherwise have been the case.

The whole scenario of working with guides is intended to make life easier and more enjoyable for us. It's important to continue to bear in mind that there's never any imposition on our free will. Final decisions always rest with us.

For those who don't accept that life continues after the death of the body, it seems that they're in for a surprise. For some, the surprise will initially – and perhaps for a long time in human terms – be unpleasant. Take the stories of Johann and Alfredo, for example.

For those who accept the continuity of life, there may also be many surprises, depending on their states of mind when they leave their bodies. Margaret Anna mentioned how heart-breaking it is to see the state of confusion in which many souls arrive into the spirit dimension – particularly those who expect to be judged and sent to 'unimaginable places of punishment'. However, whatever our state of mind when we pass, and whatever our beliefs before we go, there's immediate help available to all of us from spirit guides. In conjunction with other cooperating souls, the guides can help us to accelerate our adjustment to our new situation if we're open and responsive to help. As Margaret Anna has shown us, not all souls are.

Once we accept that there's life after the death of the body, it's natural to question what comes next. What is life in spirit really like? Margaret Anna considered that showing us her own journey, which she outlined in detail, was the best way to approach that question. Margaret Anna described how she gradually released the mental restrictions that she had acquired in her physical lifetime, and how impressions of what she had previously known came flooding back to her.

'Including,' she said, *'the notion of God, not as a separate being, but as the life force in all of us. There was to be no judgement other than that which I chose to make on myself.'*

Margaret Anna continued, throughout this book, to describe her journey in order to help us to envision our own. She told how she progressed in her attempts to help others, and she did not omit mentioning her loving reunion with her fiancé, Charles Holmes, who died so many years before her. She expanded upon her illustration of life in spirit by emphasising how much fun they have – how much joy was exuded and abounded. There were, however, words of caution. The joy and happiness are evident to, and accessible by, all; however, the states of awareness with which we leave earth and enter spirit directly affect how quickly and effectively we are able to access the joys and unconditional love of spirit. It's not always easy, but we now know that being prepared can help us to move on, to embrace spirit, and enjoy what is to come.

Margaret Anna has told a multitude of stories, in which we have seen the variety of ways in which souls have endured great distress and suffering. All of these stories have one thing in common – we punish ourselves when we close our minds, when we allow ourselves to languish in our conditioned thinking.

So there's nothing to be feared in the death of the body. Life continues in spirit. How it continues depends on how open-minded we are, how free we are from all dogmatism and rigidity of opinion, and how willing we are to receive the help that's available to us in such abundance.

It follows that the more open-minded and free from judgementalism we are on earth, the easier and more enjoyable our lives will be, and the more ready we are to continue the adventure of life in a blissful way. Writing these words reminded me that my friend, Frank, who has been so helpful to Brian, and, I'm sure, many others, said in one of his communications that he never knew the full meaning of the word 'bliss' until he had settled into his new life in spirit. (One of the meanings given to 'bliss' in my dictionary is 'perfect joy or happiness'.)

At one stage I couldn't resist asking Margaret Anna whether she had come across the bishops who treated her so humiliatingly.

Margaret Anna was magnanimous in her reply. She said, *'Yes. We have been able to laugh about our "tête-à-têtes". I haven't seen much of them. I felt I had to acknowledge that they helped me fulfil my purpose, although I didn't think so at the time. So I thanked them and left them to their own explorations.'*

Margaret Anna's answer contains an interesting point. When we look back, we can sometimes see how what we perceived to be adverse circumstances were, in the long run, actually helpful. Our reactions to them are, of course, the key to how we perceive them and what we learn from them.

I'm reminded of an Indian story about an Emperor named Akbar, and his chief minister, Birbal. One day they went hunting in a forest. Akbar broke his thumb as he was shooting. Birbal bandaged it and, as he was doing so, he tried to console Akbar by saying, 'Majesty, we never know what's good or what's bad for us.' Far from being consoled by that remark, Akbar flew into a rage and threw Birbal into a deserted well.

Akbar continued further into the forest on his own. Suddenly, a group of forest inhabitants appeared, disarmed him, and took him to their chief. In line with their custom, they were about to offer a human sacrifice to their god, and Akbar seemed to be a providential candidate. However, when the chief examined him, he noticed the bandage on his thumb and rejected him. The sacrificial offering had to be without a blemish of any kind. They let him go.

Akbar immediately ran back to the well into which he had thrown Birbal, pulled him out and begged his pardon for what he had unjustly done to him. Birbal said, 'Majesty, you have no need to ask any pardon from me. On the contrary, you did me a big favour. If you hadn't thrown me into the well, I'd have gone on into the forest with you and I'd have been sacrificed. So you see, we never know when something is good or bad for us.'

What we see as a crisis in an immediate sense may turn out to be a blessing in the long run.

There's another story – a Chinese one this time, I think – that I can't resist telling. A farmer owned a horse that he needed to till his fields. One day the horse ran away into the hills. All of his neighbours sympathised with the farmer about his bad luck.

The farmer said, 'Bad luck? Good luck? Who knows?'

A week later the horse reappeared, accompanied by a number of wild horses from the hills. This time, the farmer's neighbours congratulated him on his good luck.

Again, the farmer said, 'Bad luck? Good luck? Who knows?'

When the farmer's son was trying to tame one of the horses, he fell off its back and broke one of his legs. Again, the neighbours sympathised with the farmer on his son's bad luck and got the same reaction from him.

Some time later an army marched into the village and conscripted every able-bodied young man they found there. Because of his broken leg, the farmer's son was rejected.

Bad luck? Good luck? Who knows?

Before we completed our conversations relating to this book, Margaret Anna asked me how I felt about what she had transmitted to me.

I assured her that I felt happy, and that her experience and descriptions of life after death were very comforting. I mentioned that I had been struck in particular by the way in which she had very simply explained how we have allowed ourselves to become prisoners of our free will instead of enjoying it as the wonderful gift that it is.

Margaret Anna said, *'As you know, prisoners who are released after long prison sentences more often than not find it very difficult to adjust to the relative freedom of the outside world. The routine of institutional life – much though they may have felt trapped by it – had become the only form of freedom that they knew. I mentioned the challenge of freedom earlier. How to be free spirits – that's what all souls are faced with.'*

I hope the material in this book will prove helpful in meeting that challenge, including easing the burden of day-to-day living.

Grief

Before I finish, I'd like to talk to you a little more about grief, which I think may be the most distressing emotion of all.

Margaret Anna told the story of Jane, the young mother who succumbed to cancer. The story highlighted the distress experienced in both dimensions – that of Jane in spirit and her family on earth. I quoted Margaret Anna's description of her grief when she heard of the sudden death of her fiancé, Charles Holmes. It's worth repeating because I think it's one the most moving descriptions I have read: 'I lay in a darkened room for months, for it seemed to me as if the sunlight was too glad.' I can only imagine how wonderful her loving reunion with Charles was, not to mention its joyful affirmation of the fact that there are no goodbyes.

In my own life I have had, of course, many occasions of grief. What seems like a multitude of my friends, acquaintances and relatives have moved on, including my parents, my wife

Phyllis, my sister Mary, and my brother-in-law Mossy, who was the fourth to go of the group of five of us that I referred to in the introduction to this book.

Brian got his final diagnosis about sixteen months before his passing, and during that period he lived with the knowledge that he was on borrowed time. Because he lived on his own I was in daily contact with him, often wondering after I telephoned him at night whether he'd answer my call the next morning. At night, when I'd fall asleep watching television (as I have to admit I regularly do, even during programmes I really want to see), I'd wake up with a start, anxious that I might be too late to ring Brian. Even now, as I'm writing this, nearly six months after his passing, I still remind myself to call him – until I remember that he's not in his apartment any more to take my call. When I walk by the block of apartments where he had lived I feel a pang when I realise that there's no longer any reason for me to go in there.

After the initial shock, I wonder whether the worst part of grief is what I would call the 'missing', and all of the reminders … the empty armchair, the absence on festive occasions, little idiosyncrasies, the sense of humour, the vulnerabilities, the occasionally stubborn set of jaw … All of these are part of the togetherness of existence on earth, with all its ups and downs.

I asked Brian whether the picture I had painted of life for him after his passing was accurate. He confirmed that it was. He added, 'I miss my friends, but not my life.'

I had known some of his friends for many years; others I met during the final stages of his illness, at his funeral, and since his passing. I discovered what a wonderful group of people they are and how much they love and miss him. I hope it will be consoling for them to know that he misses and loves them, too, and that they will all meet again,

Before Brian passed on, he had signed a card that contained a photograph of himself, a quotation from one of my books that included words to effect that 'one soul is never more than a thought away from another', and an illustration of a spirit rising from a coffin, with a caption, 'I'll just be in the next room,' on top. He signed the card 'Love Brian', and asked that it should be distributed at his funeral – and to anybody who might want it. His writing was wobbly as he had become very weak at that stage and, of course, he was writing with his left hand. But he was fully conscious of what he was doing and that he wanted to do it. He has since said that one of the first things he noticed in spirit, to his delight, was that he now had his right hand back – just as it used to be.

I've used Brian's case as an example because I hope that it will be relevant for anyone who has been bereaved. I hope my son's death and subsequent passing on encourage us all to believe that we are not cut off from communication with our loved ones, and that we will meet again in joyful celebration.

In bringing up the subject of grief again, I want to shine a hopeful light on an emotion from which none of us can escape on our human journeys. I doubt if there are many people who would say that life on earth is a 'doddle'. It doesn't help much if we don't have any concept of the point of it all.

Obviously, the time I have left on earth is now very limited, even if I live to be 100, which I won't ! If I had chosen to reject the opportunity that was presented to me thirty-two years ago of communication with guides and people who had 'died', I'm trying to imagine what I'd be feeling now. I know I wouldn't be able to convince myself that there wouldn't be continuing life after physical death. I'd say I'd probably be nervous, maybe even frightened and not wanting to think of what might be waiting for me.

As things are, because I've had the privilege of having had access to so much information about what life in spirit is like, and the wonder of having whatever I want just by thinking about it and not feeling tired or ill or physically caged, with endless opportunities for exploration in whatever direction might appeal to me, there's no longer any room for fearful emotions in my consciousness in so far as the inevitable collapse of my body is concerned.

Because I'm somewhat reclusive by nature and have become more so as I have grown older, I have been hesitant about drawing attention to myself in the way I have done in this book. Yet I wouldn't like to leave the physical dimension without sharing the information that has been so generously conveyed to me by my friends in spirit. If I did, I wonder what Margaret Anna would say to me. She'd be totally understanding, I'm sure, but I'd feel I had let her down. I'd have an option to come back again, of course, and maybe choose a more extroverted personality next time round!

Anyway, it's done. I sincerely hope that the information in this book, as I have presented it to the best of my ability, will open doors for people towards more understanding of what the whole process of being born, living and dying is about and that, when the time comes to move on, they can do so in the knowledge that they will get a loving welcome into a continuing, joyful, never-ending adventure.